Volume 13   Number 1   2017

Journal of
Character Education

Jacques S. Benninga
Marvin W. Berkowitz
Editors

Jonathan M. Tirrell
Managing Editor

INFORMATION AGE
PUBLISHING

JOURNAL OF CHARACTER EDUCATION

EDITORS

Jacques S. Benninga, *California State University, Fresno*
Marvin W. Berkowitz, *University of Missouri—St. Louis*

EDITORIAL BOARD

Sheldon Berman, *Andover (MA) Public Schools*
Melinda Bier, *University of Missouri–St. Louis*
Shelley H. Billig, *RMC Research Corporation*
Ann Higgins D'Allesandro, *Fordham University*
Matthew Davidson, *Institute for Excellence and Ethics (NY)*
Maurice Elias, *Rutgers University*
Constance Flanagan, *University of Wisconsin-Madison*
Brian R. Flay, *Oregon State University*
Perry L. Glanzer, *Baylor University*
William Hansen, *Tanglewood Research*
Charles C. Haynes, *First Amendment Center*
John D. Hoge, *University of Georgia*
James Leming, *Character Evaluation Associates (FL)*
Thomas Lickona, *State University of New York–Cortland*
Marco Muñoz, *Jefferson (KY) County Public Schools*
Larry Nucci, *University of California at Berkeley*
Fritz Oser, *University of Fribourg*
Terry Pickeral, *Cascade Educational Consultants*
Clark Power, *University of Notre Dame*
Kevin Ryan, *Boston University*
Eric Schaps, *Developmental Studies Center*
Arthur Schwartz, *Widener University*
Scott Seider, *Boston University*
Bryan Sokol, *Saint Louis University*
Herbert J. Walberg, *University of Illinois at Chicago*
Lawrence J. Walker, *University of British Columbia*
Mary Williams, *George Mason University*
James Youniss, *Catholic University of America*

MANAGING EDITOR

Jonathan M. Tirrell, *Tufts University*

Journal of Character Education
Volume 13 • Number 1 • 2017

SPECIAL ISSUE
National Academies of Sciences, Engineering, and Medicine
Workshop on Approaches to the Development of Character
Part 1

MISSION STATEMENT

The *Journal of Character Education* serves an audience of researchers, policymakers, teacher educators, and school practitioners concerned with the development of positive character in young people. Character.org defines character education as efforts to help young people develop good character, which includes knowing about, caring about, and acting on core ethical values such as fairness, honesty, compassion, responsibility, and respect for self and others. The editors and Character.org view character education as a comprehensive and interdisciplinary term that reflects Character.org's Eleven Principles of Effective Character Education. These principles call on schools to address character education in their overall school climate, academic curriculum, extracurricular activities, interpersonal relationships, and school governance. These efforts are school-wide and should touch every student and all school personnel. They can include both comprehensive school reform and more specific school-based efforts such as service learning, life skills education, conflict resolution and violence prevention, social and emotional learning, education for the prevention of drug/alcohol abuse, sex education, education for civic virtue and social responsibility, and the development of moral reasoning. Of clear relevance also are multicultural education, social justice education, the ethics of environmental or technology education, religious education, and the like. The Journal will publish articles that report the results of research relevant to character education, as well as conceptual articles that provide theoretical, historical, and philosophical perspectives on the field of character education as it is broadly defined above. The Journal is also interested in more practical articles about implementation and specific programs.

Directions to Contributors

All manuscripts submitted must conform to the style of the *Publication Manual of the American Psychological Association* (APA), 6th Edition. Manuscripts must be typewritten, double-spaced throughout with 1" to 1.5" margins all around. Manuscripts typically should run between 15–25 pages in length, excluding references. All manuscripts should include an abstract of 100–150 words and a separate title page that includes the name(s) and affiliation(s) of the authors, as well as contact information for the lead author: address, phone number, fax number, and e-mail address. Following preliminary editorial review, manuscripts are sent for blind review to reviewers who have expertise in the subject of the article. The title page will be removed before the manuscript is distributed to reviewers.

Manuscripts may be submitted by e-mail to jce@umsl.edu.

APPROACHES TO THE DEVELOPMENT OF CHARACTER IN ORGANIZED OUT-OF-SCHOOL SETTINGS

Richard M. Lerner
Tufts University

Deborah Lowe Vandell
University of California–Irvine

Jonathan M. Tirrell
Tufts University

Parents, educators, youth-development practitioners, and scholars are united in an interest in identifying the contexts of youth that are associated with positive development. With increasing urgency, this interest is focused on a key indicator of positive development: *Character*. Embodied by the vision of the Reverend Dr. Martin Luther King Jr., that "my four little children will one day live in a nation where they will not be judged by the color of their skin, but by the content of their character," the growing interest in character development is predicated on the aspirations of parents and of youth-development practitioners that enhancing children's character will benefit both individuals and civil society.

Consistent with this societal emphasis, current applied developmental scholarship seeks to understand the processes through which an individual's actions in key ecological settings result in positive outcomes (Bornstein, 2015; Crosnoe & Benner, 2015; Ganong, Coleman, & Russell, 2015; Lerner, Lerner, Bowers, & Geldhof, 2015; Rubin, Bukowski, & Bowker, 2015; Vandell, Larson, Mahoney, & Watts, 2015). As explained by Vandell et al. (2015),

much of this research is framed by relational developmental systems-based models of individual ⇔ context relations (Overton, 2015), such as the bioecological model proposed by Bronfenbrenner (2005; Bronfenbrenner & Morris, 2006). The focus on using RDS-based ideas as a frame for character development research has occurred, at least in part, because of philosophical, theoretical, and empirical work that has addressed the issues of if and how attributes of character (e.g., the character virtues presented in Aristotle's *Nicomachean Ethics*, written in about 350 B.C.) promote thriving in youth while also fostering positive civic engagement and positive and valued contributions to communities (Berkowitz, 2012). Indeed, key conceptual models of character development (e.g., Lerner & Callina, 2014; Nucci, 2016) conceptualize character as attributes of an individual's relations with his or her social context that involve coherently "doing the right thing" across time and place to provide mutually, positive benefits to both person and setting.

The emphasis on character as involving mutually beneficial relations between an indi-

Journal of Character Education, Volume 13(1), 2017, pp. v–x
ISSN 1543-1223

vidual and his or her community context (represented as individual ⇔ context relations) has been a basis for the growing interest in studying character development in key settings for youth development, such as families, schools, and organized out-of-school (OST) activities. OST settings are important to add to families and schools as a key developmental context of youth development. Not only do millions of school-age youth spend substantial amounts of time in organized OST activities, including sports, faith-based initiatives, and programs such as 4-H or Scouting, but these activities often afford unique opportunities for sustained engagement that is motivated by the interests of youth (Larson, 2000). In addition, researchers have found organized OST activities to impact character-related attributes (e.g., positive purpose; kindness, generosity, or contribution to others; diligence, perseverance, or grit; and honesty, integrity, or fairness) as well as affect several academic, socioemotional, behavioral, noncognitive, and physical indicators of positive development that may be either moderators or covariates of character development (Vandell et al., 2015).

This research has attracted the burgeoning interest of practitioners and applied developmental scientists (e.g., Ettekal, Callina, & Lerner, 2015; Wang, Batanova, Ferris, & Lerner, 2016). Reflective of this interest was a workshop convened by the National Academies of Sciences, Engineering, and Medicine in July 2016 to review research and practice relevant to the development of character, with a particular focus on ideas that can support the adults who develop and run out-of-school programs. The Committee on Defining and Measuring Character and Character Education was appointed to plan the workshop: Deborah Vandell (chair), Catherine Bradshaw, Lucy Friedman, Ellen Gannet, Stephanie Jones, Richard M. Lerner, Velma McBride Murry, and Jennifer Brown Urban. Alexandra Beatty served as the senior program officer from the National Academy. The committee recognized that there are many definitions of character and many ways of describing the objectives for

programs that aim to help young people develop positive attributes. The committee members noted that, whereas good character is in one sense easy to recognize—in people who are responsible, honorable, and emotionally healthy, for example—the words used to describe it may seem to imply stances on complex questions. For example, some people who study these issues use the tools of biology and psychology to understand individual differences, whereas others focus on questions of culture, gender, and power relationships to explore the roles young people are asked to emulate.

Although thorough exploration of these complex issues was beyond the scope of the workshop, the committee was able to focus on obtaining an overview of the available academic research and structuring discussions with presenters who reflected a variety of expertise and perspectives. The committee members also had the goal of meeting the needs of practitioners, particularly those involved in out-of-school programs, and of encouraging researchers and practitioners to learn from one another. The committee designed the workshop to explore four themes:

- defining and understanding character,
- identifying what works in developing character,
- implementing development strategies and evaluating outcomes, and
- measuring character.

The committee commissioned several papers and planned sessions that allowed participants ample time to engage with the authors and one another, and to consider ways the material presented could apply in their own work. A summary of the workshop was published by the National Academies of Science, Engineering, and Medicine (2017), and can be found at https://www.nap.edu/catalog/24684/approaches-to-the-development-of-character-proceedings-of-a-workshop.

In this two-part special issue, we bring together the voices of eminent scholars and practitioners who participated in the June 2016 National Academies of Sciences workshop, "Approaches to the Development of Character," to address in greater depth and detail the four above-noted themes. All articles underwent additional peer review and revision prior to acceptance into the special issue. In Part 1 of the special issue, three primary articles and three commentaries address the definition of character, effective practices in character education, and the role of OST programs in character development, respectively. In Part 2 of this special issue, three primary articles and two commentaries address the implementation and evaluation of character development programs and issues related to the measurement of character and its development. A final commentary by Alexandra Beatty of the National Academies of Sciences, Engineering, and Medicine reflects on the importance of fortifying the research on character development at a time of urgent challenges that test character, and the value of weaving these ideas into activities that naturally engage young people's curiosity and enthusiasm.

Accordingly, in the first part of this special issue, Larry Nucci conceptualizes character as a developmental system embedded within the self-system. Using a relational developmental systems (RDS)-based perspective, he views the character system as including four components. The first three components consist of basic moral cognition (as described within domain theory), other regarding, and self-regarding social emotional capacity. These three components comprise "moral wellness." The fourth component "moral critical social engagement" defines mature moral character. Nucci emphasizes that character and the context are mutually constitutive and continuously coacting. Character is captured through its coherence within and across contexts rather than consistency of actions or moral choices.

In their commentary, Kristina Schmid Callina and Richard M. Lerner focus on the idea of coherence as it applies to understanding character development, education, and assessment.

They propose that coherence may be understood in at least three, interrelated ways: as the appropriate application of morality to a particular situation; as employing the right virtue, in the right amount, at the right time (Aristotle's concept of phronesis); and as an integrated system of moral concepts. In his commentary, Robert E. McGrath focuses on Nucci's equation of character with moral functioning. He discusses his research, indicating that inquisitiveness and self-control are indicators of character even when not used to support moral ends, so long as they are not used to support immoral ones. In addition, he suggests that Nucci's model should be expanded to outline competing considerations that enter into moral decision-making.

The second primary paper, written by Marvin W. Berkowitz, Melinda C. Bier, and Brian McCauley, summarizes the findings from eight reviews of the literature on the effectiveness of character education programs. From this work, they develop a conceptual framework of six foundational character educational principles (PRIMED) and use it as an organizational structure for the 42 character education practices. In addition, they provide a comparison of practices that support academic achievement and those fostering character development, and show substantial overlap in effective academic and character practices.

In her commentary, Camille A. Farrington extends the discussion provided by Berkowitz, Bier, and McCauley by addressing the question of how child and youth environments might "build character." She uses both theoretical work and empirical studies in other disciplines (e.g., neuroscience, cognitive science, social psychology, developmental psychology, sociology, philosophy) to theorize about potential processes whereby school practices develop character in children and adolescents. She proposes that 10 particular "developmental experiences"—specific opportunities provided for young people to act and reflect—are means through which settings influence the development of character and equip children and youth to build toward agency, an integrated identity, and a set of competencies that support success in young adulthood. Finally, she notes some potential alignments with Berkowitz and colleagues' PRIMED framework.

The paper by Deborah A. Moroney and Elizabeth Devaney then reviews the evidence on staff practices and quality programs that foster character development through social and emotional learning. Describing the state of the OST workforce, and barriers and opportunities to adding social and emotional learning to their job description, the authors provide an overview of the literature on the characteristics of staff practices that yield positive youth outcomes and the readiness of the OST workforce to implement intentional opportunities for social and emotional learning. They explore current and potential future efforts in the field to prepare staff to incorporate practices that support social and emotional learning.

In the second volume of the special issue, Joseph A. Durlak reviews literature that emphasizes how both research findings and practical applications have confirmed the fundamental importance of program implementation in the spread of successful character education interventions. He discusses some of the multiple factors that can enhance or impede effective implementation, and presents a framework that illustrates the multiple steps that should be followed to increase the chances that a program will be put to a fair test in a new setting. Using findings from character development interventions to illustrate various points, the author notes that a collaborative partnership between researchers and practitioner is critical to effective implementation.

Jennifer Brown Urban and William M. Trochim discuss how character development practitioners, researchers, and funders might think about evaluation, how evaluation fits into their work, and what needs to happen in order to sustain evaluative practices. They present a view of evaluation whereby evaluation is not just seen as something that is applied at a program level, but is an endeavor that considers the ecologies and systems within which pro-

grams are embedded. The authors present strategies for enhancing evaluation practices at the organizational (macro) level as well as strategies for enhancing evaluation practice at the program (micro) level.

Noel A. Card provides an overview of the methodological issues involved in measuring constructs relevant to character development and education. He discusses the three fundamental psychometric properties of measurement: reliability, validity, and equivalence. He emphasizes that developing and evaluating measures to ensure evidence of all three psychometric properties has substantial impact on the quality of character development and education research. In his commentary, Clark McKown notes that, if researchers and practitioners want character and social and emotional learning skills to be addressed in schools and youth development programs, they had better assess those skills. To build on the ideas of Card, McKown raises four points. First, advancing assessment in the field requires a vigorous pursuit of conceptual clarity. Second, the field will benefit from efforts specifically creating assessments designed for practice; these efforts should include consideration of how assessment data are interpreted and used. Third, clarity is needed about the purposes for assessing character and social and emotional learning. Fourth, the method of assessment is a critical but underappreciated consideration, because different methods of assessment are suited to measuring different dimensions of character and social and emotional learning. In her commentary, Nancy L. Deutsch focuses on the ways in which social scientific knowledge represents human constructions of the world and the implications of this stance for the measurement of character. She considers how context influences those constructions and the need for researchers to more purposefully engage with questions of construct (in)stability across contexts both within and between people. She points to the need to expand developmental scientists' methodological tool box to include multiple quantitative and qualitative methods.

CONCLUSIONS

Collectively, we believe these articles will further advance understanding of character development as well as inform best practices for character assessment, measurement, and promotion in youth. As coeditors of this special issue, we hope that readers find this collection of articles both informative and inspiring.

REFERENCES

Berkowitz, M.W. (2012). Moral and character education. In K. R. Harris, S. Graham, & T. Urdan (Eds.), *APA educational psychology handbook. Vol. 2: Individual differences and contextual factors* (pp. 247–264). Washington, DC: American Psychological Association.

Bornstein, M. M. (2015). Children's parent. In M. H. Bornstein & T. Leventhal (Eds.), *Ecological settings and processes: Vol. 4. Handbook of child psychology and developmental science* (7th ed., pp. 55–132). Hoboken, NJ: Wiley.

Bronfenbrenner, U. (2005). *Making human beings human: Bioecological perspectives on human development*. Thousand Oaks, CA: SAGE.

Bronfenbrenner, U., & Morris, P. A. (2006). The bioecological model of human development. In W. Damon & R. M. Lerner (Eds.) & R. M. Lerner (Vol. Ed.), *Handbook of child psychology: Vol. 1. Theoretical models of human development* (6th ed., pp. 793–828). Hoboken, NJ: Wiley.

Ettekal, A. V., Callina, K. S., & Lerner, R. M. (2015). The promotion of character through youth development programs. *Journal of Youth Development, 10*(3), 6–13.

Ganong, L., Coleman, M., & Russell, L. T. (2015). Children in diverse families. In M. H. Bornstein & T. Leventhal (Eds.), *Ecological settings and processes: Vol. 4. Handbook of child psychology and developmental science* (7th ed., pp. 133–174). Hoboken, NJ: Wiley.

Crosnoe, R., & Benner, A. D. (2015). Children at school. In M. H. Bornstein & T. Leventhal (Eds.), *Ecological settings and processes: Vol. 4 Handbook of child psychology and developmental science* (7th ed., pp. 268–204). Hoboken, NJ: Wiley.

Larson, R. W. (2000). Toward a psychology of positive youth development. *American Psychologist, 55*(1), 170–183. http://dx.doi.org/10.1037/0003-066X.55.1.170

Lerner, R. M., & Callina, K. S. (2014). The study of character development: Towards tests of a relational developmental systems model. *Human Development, 57*(6), 322–346.

Lerner, R. M., Lerner, J. V., Bowers, E., & Geldhof, G. J. (2015) Positive youth development and relational developmental systems. In W. F. Overton & P. C. Molenaar (Eds.), *Theory and method: Vol. 1. Handbook of child psychology and developmental science* (7th ed., pp. 607–651). Hoboken, NJ: Wiley.

National Academies of Sciences, Engineering, and Medicine. (2017). *Approaches to the development of character: Proceedings of a workshop.* Washington, DC: The National Academies Press. https://doi.org/10.17226/24684

Nucci, L. (2016, July). *Character: A multi-faceted developmental system.* Paper presented at The National Academy of Sciences, Engineering, and Medicine Workshop on Approaches to the Development of Character, Washington, DC.

Overton, W. F. (2015). Process and relational developmental systems. In W. F. Overton & P. C. M. Molenaar (Eds.), *Handbook of child psychology and developmental science: Vol. 1. Theory and method* (7th ed., pp. 9–62). Hoboken, NJ: Wiley.

Rubin, K. H., Bukowski, W. M., & Bowker, J. C. (2015). Children in peer groups. In M. H. Bornstein & T. Leventhal (Eds.), *Ecological settings and processes: Vol. 4. Handbook of child psychology and developmental science* (7th ed., pp. 175–222). Hoboken, NJ: Wiley.

Vandell, D. L., Larson, R. W., Mahoney, J. L., & Watts, T. W. (2015). Children's organized activities. In M. H. Bornstein & T. Leventhal (Vol. Eds.), *Handbook of child psychology and developmental science: Vol. 4. Ecological settings and processes* (7th ed., pp. 305–344). Hoboken, NJ: Wiley.

Wang, J., Batanova, M., Ferris, K. A., & Lerner, R. M. (Eds). (2016). Character development: Tests of relational developmental systems models [Special issue]. *Research in Human Development, 13*(2).

CHARACTER
A Multifaceted Developmental System

Larry Nucci
University of California, Berkeley

Character is a developmental system embedded within the self-system. This Relational Developmental Systems (RDS) view is in juxtaposition with virtue theory and accounts of character in terms of moral identity. The character system includes 4 components 3 of which: basic moral cognition (as described within domain theory); other regarding; and self-regarding social emotional capacity, comprise "moral wellness." The fourth component "moral critical social engagement" defines mature moral character. The fourth component rests on the willingness of individuals to employ their moral reasoning to question the conventions of society and their personal moral positions. It also entails responsive engagement in moral discourse with others of diverging social positions and moral perspectives to arrive at shared morally defensible positions. This RDS perspective views character and the context as mutually constitutive and continuously interacting. Character is captured through its coherence within and across contexts rather than consistency of actions or moral choices.

Most people, including skeptics of the character construct, have a sense of what Martin Luther King (King, Carson, & Carson, 2007) meant when he uttered the famous lines in his "I have a dream" speech looking forward to the day when his children would "not be judged by the color of their skin but by the content of their character." It is also worth noting that King would prioritize character as the aspect of persons most central to their evaluation. Nonetheless, social scientists and educators are hard pressed to offer a common definition of character, and an important core of researchers in moral education beginning with Lawrence Kohlberg (Kohlberg & Mayer, 1972) have challenged the scientific validity and educational utility of the character construct. In the face of these challenges, this paper will offer a coherent view of character that will bring together the disparate strands of current work in the areas of moral development and moral education, social and emotional learning, and character formation. This argument will draw from the work of several people (e.g., Berkowitz 2012; Berkowitz & Bier, 2014; Lerner & Callina, 2014; Wainryb & Pasupathi, 2015) to make the case that the study of character and its assessment must

• **Correspondence concerning this article should be addressed to:** Larry Nucci, nucci@berkeley.edu

ISSN 1543-1223

employ a multimethod approach that views character as a multifaceted dynamic developmental system rather than a search for traits or entities within the person.

LIMITATIONS IN CURRENT DEFINITIONS OF CHARACTER

Character as Virtues

Traditionally, character has been defined in terms of a set of traits or virtues (e.g., Carr, 2008) that emerge from socialization practices that foster habit formation and internalization of culturally valued qualities that guide behaviors (Sokol, Hammond, & Berkwowitz, 2010). There are several fundamental problems with this traditional approach to character. The first is the lack of agreement across cultures and historical periods as to which qualities count as virtues (Sokol et al., 2010). A humorous example of the variability in the identification of virtues was provided by Daniel Lapsley (1996). Lapsley compared the virtues listed in his own elementary school report card against the list of core values for character education established in 1988 by the American Association for Curriculum Development (ASCD). He found that the only value that overlapped on the two lists was courtesy. Moreover, he reported that the list offered by the American Association for Curriculum Development in 1988 left out 9 of the 11 core values compiled by the same organization in 1929. A more systematic recent historical analysis by Robert McGrath (2016) found that of the five primary virtues identified by Plato only one (courage) made it into the list of 16 primary virtues identified by Aristotle, and only one of the virtues maintained by Aristotle (justice) made it onto the list of seven core virtues identified by Catholicism.

In addition to the variability in the identification of virtue, attempts to define character in terms of virtues run contrary to evidence demonstrating that people are by and large inconsistent in their application of virtues. The well-known studies by Hartshorne and May in the 1920s for example, found that people were

honest in some contexts and dishonest in others. Character as a set of virtues was nonexistent, according to Hartshorne and May (1928) as people appear to behave differently as a function of context. Contemporary virtue philosophers have attempted to address these short-comings by appealing to the application of judgments in context through "practical expertise" (Annas, 2011) that selects which element of virtue to apply, or through a modification in the definition of virtue that allows for partial realization of an ideal within varying contexts. These "teeny bits of virtue" (Curzer, 2016, 2018) function by capturing the larger trajectory of the virtues that comprise an individual's character. Such adjustments in virtue theory, however, are acknowledgments that the core of moral action lies in the judgments made within context rather than static abstract qualities thought to define the person. In concert with this view, developmental psychologists (Lerner & Callina, 2014) have argued that defining virtues as traits engages in a "split metaphor" in which qualities of the person are treated as discrete and apart from the context.

Moral Identity

Researchers in the field of moral education who have moved away from reference to virtue have instead focused upon what they refer to as the "moral self" or "moral identity" (Blasi, 2005; Hardy & Carlo, 2005; Krettenauer & Hertz, 2015; Lapsley & Stey, 2014). A common strategy adopted within this area of inquiry has been to study the life histories and shared features of moral exemplars. The notion here is that some people hold morality closer to the core of their identity than do others. Critics of this assumption (e.g., Nucci, 2004; Wainryb & Pasupathi, 2015) have noted that moral exemplars turn out to be not so different from the rest of us in terms of their concerns for morality, once you exam the totality of their lives. That is to say that with the exception of the small percentage of people who are psychopaths, current evidence suggests that all people care about morality. Moreover, people care about how they view themselves as moral people. In a recent comprehensive review of the research on moral identity, Lapsley (2016) reports that moral categories are more readily accessible than competence traits and dominate our impression formation. As suggested in M.L. King's quote, it is moral character that is most distinctive about identity and what we care most about in others.

Variations in the centrality of moral identity, however, have less impact. The outcomes of 3 decades of studies exploring self-report measures of the centrality individuals place on possessing and enacting moral values has uncovered individual differences in the expected direction (enactment of prosocial actions abstaining from antisocial behavior) (Lapsley, 2016). However, the differences are relatively small and not uniquely associated with moral identity as the explanatory variable (Krettenauer & Hertz, 2015).

The focus upon identity has stemmed from the mistaken notion that moral motivation comes from the desire to act in accordance with one's view of oneself as a moral being. This viewpoint runs the risk of reducing morality to self-interest, and undermines the motivational force that is inherent in knowing what is the "right' thing to do (Nucci, 2004). Where people appear to differ is in their reading of social contexts, their degree of social and emotional regulation, and other factors that impact their actions within particular contexts. The concern for moral identity as Wainryb (2011) has elegantly shown emerges most powerfully as people confront the consequences of their own wrong-doing rather than as a motive for action. Paradoxically, an overconcern for morality has its own downside in the form of moral zealotry. The philosopher Susan Wolf (2001) has written critically of "moral saints" lacking in balance and incomplete as persons.

Toward a Definition of Character

The emphasis on identity is grounded in the reasonable insight that concerns about moral-

ity are connected to one's sense of self (Blasi, 2005). As will be outlined below, current evidence is consistent with a definition of character as a partial system operating within the self as a whole. The self-system includes our overall sense of agency (Proulx & Chandler 2009, Deci & Ryan, 2014) and unique personal identity (Nucci, 2014). The overall self-system also includes such things as our gender or ethnic identity, and sense of ourselves as productive members of the family or society. What we mean as character borrowing directly from Marvin Berkowitz (2012, p. 248) is "the composite of those characteristics of the individual that directly motivate and enable him or her to act as a moral agent." Moral agency as defined by Wainryb (Pasupathi & Wainryb, 2010) refers to people's understandings and experience of themselves as agents—people whose morally relevant actions are grounded in their own mental states, goals, beliefs and emotions. Moral agency, as will be discussed below, is a critical component of what is referred to here to as basic moral wellness. Moral agency emerges throughout childhood both through reflections on positive actions, but also very powerfully as children account for their own harmful actions and the harmful actions of others (Recchia, Wainryb, Bourne, & Pasupathi, 2015). Experiences of trauma, and the engagement in acts of violence impact and disrupt the formation and status of moral agency (Wainryb, 2011).

As discussed here, however, character is not simply a collection of components contributing to moral agency as Berkowitz' (2012) definition leaves open as a possibility. What is being proposed instead is a system of interrelating partial structures that inform and impact one another within contexts. These component systems are themselves operating within a reciprocal dynamic relationship with the context. This definition of character conforms to the Relational Developmental Systems (RDS) metatheory offered by Lerner (Lerner, 2006; Lerner & Callina, 2014) and Overton (2015). This article is not the context in which to fully review this metatheory. A key aspect of the dynamic developmental systems metatheory for our understanding of character is that it views the relationship between the individual and the context as in continuous mutually constitutive relationship rather than a notion of the interaction between the individual and context as accounting for a proportion of the variance. This is depicted within Figure 1. Thus notions of character as virtues that exist independent of their enactment within a context are meaningless. This holds equally true for presumed structures of moral cognition. A dynamic developmental systems view of character is also much more in keeping with the latter of work of Piaget (1985) in which he focused upon processes of equilibration than in his earlier work when he was preoccupied with an account of structures and stages. Accordingly, the present discussion of how to view morality in context will emphasize the activity of coordinations of competing elements within contexts (Nucci, Turiel, & Roded, 2017; Turiel, 2002), rather than a focus upon static definitions of stages or levels of moral reasoning (Kohlberg, 1984).

A second aspect of this metatheory is that we can take snapshot views of the person or context within a given moment or period of ontogenesis that will help to track or measure moral development and character as long as we understand these to be moments in the course of microgenetic and ontogenetic development, rather than reified and frozen entities (virtues, traits) or structures. Thus, what we should be looking for in terms of character is not consistency across contexts, but coherence (Lerner & Callina, 2014). It is not a matter of acting in the same (consistent) way (e.g., "honest") irrespective of the situation, but in a manner that is morally sensible (coherent) across situations. In addition, what is meant by character is never a finished product, but is continuously evolving. Finally, the notion of a dynamic relationship between the person and the context means that as we look over time what we will see is evidence not just of the impact of the context on the person, but the impact of the person on the context. This is not generally the object of research on character per se. However, it is argued here that a comprehensive understanding of character entails the systematic analysis of the role of people in transforming society. Taken seriously, this has implications for the goals of character education in terms of moral citizenship.

Finally, what this means in terms of methods is that we will need to understand the difference between snapshot views of the person in one moment in time in which we ignore context, but simply try to measure, assess or describe, the structure of the person's character at that moment, and the more comprehensive

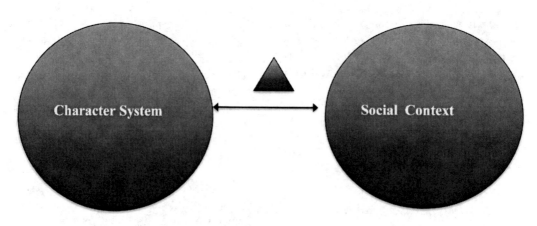

FIGURE 1
Character and Context as Interpenetrating and in Dynamic Relationship

look at the person in relationship to the context and over extended periods of time.

THE COMPONENTS OF CHARACTER AND CONTEMPORARY RESEARCH

Let us turn then to an analysis of the basic components of what collectively contribute to and comprise "character." There are four basic components. These are presented in Table 1. The first three components collectively comprise what is referred to here as basic moral wellness. Wellness connotes normative moral functioning, but also includes the assumption that establishing moral well-being is an ongoing process that requires active attention and nurturing. The three components of moral wellness are: (1) basic moral cognition, (2) other regarding social emotional capacities and skills such as empathy, and perspective-taking, and (3) self-regarding capacities for executive control and self-regulation of emotions and desires. This third component is employed both in the enactment of moral actions, and in the completion of nonmoral tasks that require steadfast commitment and engagement. In other places this steadfast commitment to the completion of nonmoral tasks has been referred to as "performance character" (Davidson, Lickona, & Khmelkov, 2008). These three components of basic moral wellness map onto the aspects of character identified by Sokol, Hammond, and Berkowitz (2010). The present model includes a fourth component, which is the discourse and communication skills and orientation for principled

moral change at the social level. This fourth component is not generally included within discussions of moral character. However, the case being made here is that the standard view of character does not account for the interpenetration of the person with the context. An RDS view of character would account for how persons as moral actors may impact the social context. Inclusion of this aspect of character is also consistent with comprehensive views of development that attend to the sociogenetic component along with micro and onto-genetic aspects of development (Saxe & Esmonde, 2012). It also allows for coherent inclusion of the work being done on moral purpose as an aspect of character formation and expression (Damon, 2009). Figure 2 represents the relationship between this character system and the self-system as a whole. It illustrates how character is connected with moral identity and agency as aspects of one's total sense of self, as well as how the self-regarding (performance) component of character can link up with other aspects of identity such as academics or sports performance.

In this analysis, "social and emotional learning" (SEL) is viewed as a contributor to character rather than viewing character as a direct outcome of SEL. Social and emotional learning refers to the emergence of basic emotional competencies, and skills such as emotion recognition and emotion regulation that are essential to basic moral mental health and moral functioning. This is consistent with the role of SEL in relationship to morality and character as discussed by Maurice Elias and his colleagues in their chapter in the *Handbook*

TABLE 1
Components of the Character System

| **Basic Moral Wellness** |
| Reasoning: Moral, conventional, personal domains |
| Other regarding SEL capacities: empathy, emotion recognition, emotion regulation, perspective-taking (theory of mind) |
| Self-regarding SEL capacities: Self-regulation, emotion regulation, executive control |
| **Moral Critical Social Engagement** (Discourse/communication skills for responsive engagement and moral evaluation of self and society; "moral purpose") |

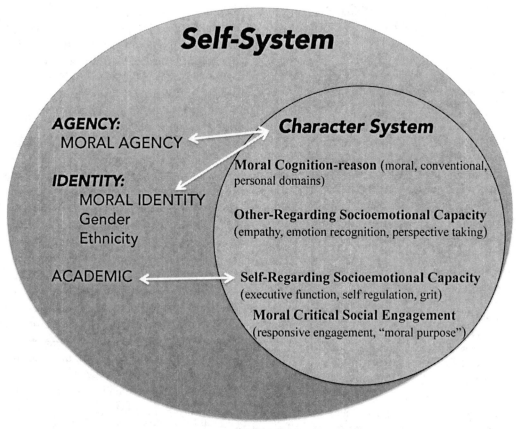

FIGURE 2
The Character System Within the Self-System

of Moral and Character Education (Elias, Parker, Kash, Weissberg, & O'Brien, 2008).

MORALITY AND MORAL COGNITION

Character is at its core about the engagement in moral choices. The notion of character is not simply that people prefer the moral option, or are emotionally drawn to the moral option, but that the person willfully elects to act in the moral direction. We do not attribute character, for example, to bees that instinctively sacrifice their lives for the hive, or to someone who accidentally disrupts a crime. This is not to suggest that a person of character would have

to ponder whether or not it is right to engage in unprovoked harm, or deliberate extensively over whether or not to help a person in need. Moral decisions, especially those made in highly familiar contexts may require little active deliberation (Narvaez & Lapsley, 2005; Turiel, 2010). However, moral judgments often entail weighing what is morally right against other personal considerations, or social expectations.

Understanding the development of the capacity to generate moral decisions within context has been the focus of research in what is referred to as social cognitive domain theory (Smetana, Jambon, & Ball, 2014). Domain theory draws a distinction between the development of judgments about morality (issues of fairness, welfare, and rights) and concepts of societal convention (consensually determined norms of a given social system), and matters that fall within the personal domain of privacy and personal choice (Smetana et al., 2014). Concepts within each domain follow independent courses of development, accounting for qualitatively differing aspects of social experience (Nucci, 2001; Turiel, 1983). Contextualized social contexts may be multifaceted, including elements from morality and considerations of social convention and/or personal needs and preferences. Decision-making in such multifaceted contexts may draw on concepts from more than one domain requiring cross-domain coordination (Smetana et al., 2014).

Character formation is thus impacted by development within domains as well as the capacity to coordinate competing considerations across domains. From this standpoint, Kohlberg's (1984) stage theory may be best thought of as a description of age-typical cross-domain coordination applied to the scenarios employed within his assessments. The inconsistencies reported in the Kohlbergian research program reflect individual differences in development within domains, and individual variations in the prioritization of moral and nonmoral considerations in varying contexts (Nucci, 2001). These nonmoral considerations include the assumptions people make about the facts or information relevant to a decision. For example, people who assume that a fertilized human egg is a human life that is to be accorded personhood will view abortion as the immoral act of murder. These assumptions are informed by science, but also by religious belief or cultural tradition.

The domain theoretical framework does not define moral development in terms of stages, and does not dismiss the impact of context simply as content for moral decision-making. Moral judgments are inexorably bound up in context. This makes the assessment of moral growth and the identification of character more challenging. As children get older their moral judgments become more comprehensive. However, there is no end point in which adults apply moral principles across all contexts independent of competing nonmoral considerations. (For a recent comprehensive discussion of these issues see Turiel & Nucci, 2018) The contextual multidomain nature of the application of morality to lived situations is why any definition of character must be framed in terms of coherence in moral judgments rather than context independent consistency. As stated above coherence refers to the rational connection among contextualized moral judgments and actions as seen from the vantage point of the actor rather than the similarity in actions within a given type of situation as seen from the point of view of an observer.

The definition of morality as centered around issues of justice and human welfare is consistent with the cognitive developmental tradition of Piaget and Kohlberg. It is also consistent with the sociocognitive framework for understanding character proposed by Lapsley (2016). However, it has come under criticism in recent years by proponents of intuitionist moral psychology (Haidt, 2001, 2012). Within this view, there are several moralities that emerge from evolutionary selection and socialization: care/harm, fairness, liberty/oppression, loyalty/betrayal, authority, sanctity. Moral decision-making according to Haidt (2001) is the outcome of emotionally driven intuitions, and that reasoning serves as after the fact rationalization rather than a source of moral decisions. Responses to Haidt's (2012) intuitionist psychology have come from several sources. First, are cognitive psychologists who argue that Haidt has misrepresented the relationship between rapid processing of deeply understood or well-rehearsed concepts or decisions, such as judgments about unprovoked harm that are constructed through interactions in early childhood, with innate emotionally driven reactions (Narveaz & Lapsley, 2005; Turiel, 2010). Second, he has underplayed and misrepresented the rational expressions of potential harm that people offer in some of the contexts such as brother-sister incest that he describes as cases of moral dumfounding (Jacobson, 2012). Perhaps more importantly, his mentor, Richard Shweder, has criticized Haidt's position as misunderstanding the rational requirements of any moral code. Morality, according to Shweder, is not simply a taste or preference, but needs to appeal to reason for its authority (Nucci, 2015). This final point is consistent with other critics who have noted that Haidt's identification of multiple presumably equivalent moralities leads to relativism in which there is no basis for deciding what is right beyond consensus, authority or preference (Blum, 2013).

OTHER REGARDING SOCIAL EMOTIONAL CAPACITY

The second component of character is comprised of the social emotional capacities for engaging the motives and needs of others. This includes the capacity for empathy (Eisenberg et al., 2002; Saarni, 1997), the ability to accurately read the emotions of others (Saarni, 1997, 2007), and perspective-taking (Martin, Sokol, & Elfers, 2008). These components provide the inputs for the universal capacity of human beings to generate moral judgments about harm and human welfare (Sokol et al., 2010). Disruptions in normative development negatively impact the development of empathy and related emotional competencies. As Wainryb's (2011) work has shown, for example, the capacity for moral agency, which is the ownership of one's moral actions and capacity to positively benefit from self-review of one's own actions causing harm to others, is seriously damaged by direct exposure to violence. Research on school based SEL programs emerged initially from efforts directed largely at ameliorating or overcoming the deficiencies in children's home lives and communities that undermine these basics for moral and social functioning. More recently, however, SEL has been viewed as a means of optimizing these emotional competencies (Elias et al., 2014) and is offered to all students. This approach is concordant with the notion of moral wellness being offered here in which normative moral functioning and character development need to be nurtured rather than viewed as an inevitable outcome of development.

SELF-REGARDING SOCIAL EMOTIONAL CAPACITIES

Character is more than the capacity for judgment of the right thing to do, it is the propensity to act on that judgment. This has often been mischaracterized as a problem of moral motivation (Nucci, 2004). The authors of research and theory on moral identity, for example, offered the desire to maintain coherence between one's actions and one's moral identity as the motive force behind moral behavior (Lapsely, 2016). Morality, however, is intrinsically motivating (Nucci, 2004). Once a decision is reached regarding what is the right course of action, that decision is its own motivation. Engaging in moral action, however, requires supporting personal strengths and socioemotional skills. This collection of capacities is core component of moral agency.

Moral agency is also sustained by the normative development within a personal domain of privacy and prerogative (Nucci, 2014). Personal issues are such things as ones choice of friends, the content of one's diary or correspondence, and aspects of personal appearance such as clothing choices. The exact content of what gets defined as personal will be impacted by culture. However, claims to a personal area of privacy and choice is grounded in the human need for the construction of selfhood and individuality (Nucci, 2014). Cultural psychologists who initially questioned the universality of a personal domain now agree that it is a component of persons in all cultures (Miller & Bland, 2014). There is also now extensive evidence that the pattern of emergence of the personal in normative development is seen across cultures as adolescents differentiate themselves and parents relinquish control over decisions in the personal area to their adolescent children (Smetana, 2010). The development of the personal is intrinsic to the construction of personal autonomy, self-determination (Deci & Ryan, 2014) and the capacity to extend compassion and moral empathy (Nucci, 2004).

Often doing the right thing comes at a cost. In some cases those costs, such as losing one's job or health, may be sufficiently high as to lead to a rational choice to prioritize self-interest over the morally right thing to do. Wainryb's (2011) interviews with child soldiers in Colombia uncovered several instances in which young teenagers were ordered by superiors to kill an unarmed opponent. In those cases the failure to act in the "moral" direction, may be understood as emerging from the coordination of moral and nonmoral factors such that morality is evaluated as secondary. This is also the case in situations where the perceived benefits or needs met by the nonmoral choice outweigh morality, such as in extramarital relationships involving love between one member of a marriage and another person outside of the marriage. Here again, the coordination of moral and nonmoral factors may be such that morality is secondary to the personal. (The salience of morality is this example, may also be minimized if the affair is secret, and the spouse presumably unharmed.) In both cases, it is not simply a case of will power or external motivators, it is simply that morality is not always primary. This is the reason that any account of character has to look at coherence and not consistency.

What is meant by character, however, is acting in the moral direction precisely when doing so competes with other goals, or comes at some cost. It means for example, not shoplifting when the opportunity presents itself, or helping someone in need even if it is inconvenient to do so. The third component of character is the capacity for self-regulation and follow-through. This is the subject of research on emotion regulation (Thompson, 2014) and executive function (Zelazo, Mueller, Douglas, & Marcovitch, 2003). Emotion regulation allows for the person to act on the basis of

rational choice, rather than the heat of the moment. Executive function serves to enable the coordination of cross-domain considerations (Richardson et al., 2012), and enhance impulse control (Kerr & Zelazo, 2004). Current research on mindfulness indicates that it contributes toward the development of capacities for executive function in children and adolescents.

More recently, work on "grit" suggests an avenue for exploring personal willingness and propensity for moral follow through. As defined by Duckworth (2016) grit is the combined capacity for passion and perseverance of long-term goals. Grit is normally associated with academic or personal achievement in areas such as the arts, athletics or business that require sustained effort in the face of obstacles or challenges. Grit would most readily be viewed as a component of performance character. It is not clear whether one can apply grit as a construct to morality. The construct of grit may help us to understand the commitment made to addressing injustices that we see in moral exemplars such as M. L. King, but also in the many youth who remain moral in the context of strong countervailing environmental challenges of poverty and systemic violence. It is possible that research on purpose may be linked to the notion of grit among individuals who elect to engage in community building or social justice work at some personal cost (Damon & Colby, 2015). However, we need to also be careful about conflating character with supererogation.

NICE IS NOT ENOUGH: DISCOURSE SKILLS FOR RESPONSIVE ENGAGEMENT, PURPOSE AND AN ORIENTATION FOR PRINCIPLED MORAL CHANGE

The components I have listed thus far account for the conventional notions of character as well as what Kohlberg (1984) referred to as conventional morality. They describe the development of the person who will operate morally in everyday life. The problem with this account is that it allows for the person of character who will live quite happily within a culture or society with structural inequalities or structural practices, such as slavery, that are themselves immoral. This is no idle concern as our own cultural history makes evident. Using the normal language of character we would be hard pressed to argue that the people living during those times were any less moral than we are in a period overtly struggling with issues of racial equality. Kohlberg (1984) attempted to account for the emergence of people whose morality transcended the norms of their cultural period as having reached a stage of development he referred to as postconventional principled moral reasoning. Unfortunately, the evidence for such an orientation as a structural developmental stage of moral development is weak (Gibbs, 2013). However, there is ample evidence from history as well as from contemporary cross-cultural research that resistance to unfair practices is common and especially prevalent among individuals in positions of lesser power or privilege (Turiel, 2002). Often their resistance is unrecognized because it occurs surreptitiously or remains as a viewpoint rather than expressed as overt action.

Translating personal moral opposition into a principled moral perspective, however, is something that may not be possible at an individual level. This is the argument made by philosophers such as Habermas (Habermas, Lenhardt, & Nicholsen, 1991) and in the later works of John Rawls (2001) that abstract moral principles cannot be translated into genuine moral positions in the absence of dialogue with those for whom those principles are meant to apply. To put this in more ordinary terms, men can only imagine if you will, the most fair way to construe the social world for women; in the absence of open dialogue with women they can never expect to actually get it right. Aside from the easy to imagine obstacles that men would face in trying to generate the fairest and most ethical ways to construct a world for women, any group of people in a position of relative power will fail to see at least some of the injustices of those who are not in positions of power (Turiel, 2002). Understanding the perspectives of those in subordinate positions, however, is also only part of the process in attempting to correct immoral practices at general societal level.

For the most part, our theoretical views of moral and character development operate at the level of the isolated individual, and do not include the role of the individual as a component within a larger social network. This is an error that functions in two directions. On the one hand, the focus upon ontogenesis leaves out the impact of sociohistorical components in individual development. One of my female graduate students asks how it is possible that boys who construct basic conceptions of morality in terms of fairness and human welfare in early childhood, and who grow up loving their mothers who gave them life and sustenance, can grow up to be misogynist adults? On the other hand, our focus on the individual leaves out the role that persons have in changing societal and cultural practices. Responding to these issues requires us to enlarge our view of development, and to incorporate the contributions of researchers who examine the sociogenetic line of development. The RDS metatheoretical perspective that I am suggesting that we take toward character requires that we fully integrate sociogenetic and ontogenetic lines of development in our theoretical accounts. This is exactly what Geoffrey Saxe (Saxe & Esmonde, 2012) has done in the area of math cognition, and what I propose that we incorporate into our comprehensive view of character.

Figure 3 is taken from Geoffrey Saxe's (Saxe & Esmonde, 2012) award winning book on the development of mathematics among generations of people within a small community in Papua New Guinea. What it represents are the coactions of ontogenetic and sociogenetic contributions to the microgenetic changes within an individual participating within a community of practice. What you will see in this deceptively simple representation is that the individual is not merely

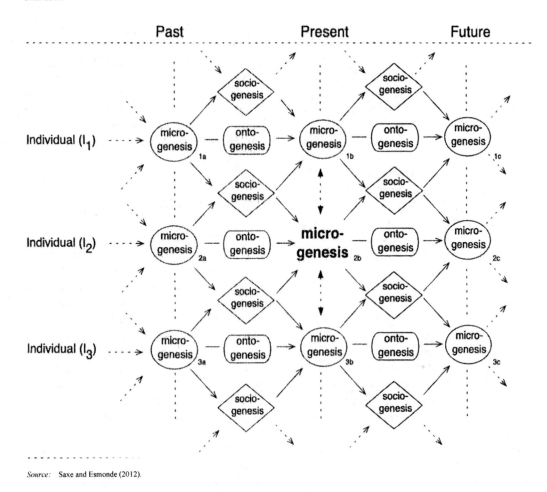

Past Present Future

Individual (I_1)

Individual (I_2)

Individual (I_3)

Source: Saxe and Esmonde (2012).

Figure 3
The Interplay Among Developmental Processes Over Time

being shaped by external inputs as in the standard view of socialization, nor is the individual merely reconstructing at an individual level what has been produced at the social level as would be the case in a Vygotskian scheme, nor is the individual engaged in a sui generis construction of reality. Instead all elements of this dynamic system (Witherington, 2011) are interpenetrating and coacting on one another. The ontogenetic line—what we might call the individual's cognitive structure—emerges within, and operates upon the social milieu of the surrounding community of practice.

Our current notions of character do not include attention to the features of persons as they interact within the discourse world of the community. There is, however, an emerging group of researchers working in collaboration with philosophers to begin to sketch out what the political philosopher Anthony Laden (2012) refers to as "responsive engagement." Responsive engagement is a form of discourse that has as its goal the location of common ground. That common ground may in fact end up being quite close to the position taken by one of the partners in a discourse, or in a third position not anticipated in by either member in advance of the discourse. What is essential for this type of discourse to count as "engaged reasoning" is that each speaker work toward finding a conceptual space that all can share, and accept as their own. "Engaged reasoning is thus reasoning together in the most robust sense of the term" (Laden, 2012, p. 171). Laden differentiates engaged reasoning from debates or efforts directed solely at persuasive argumentation. This is in the tradition of what Habermas et al. (1991) referred to as communicative discourse.

Laden's (2012) viewpoint is viewed as naïve by Jon Haidt (2012) who claims that it is basically a waste of time to try and get members of a discourse to be open-minded and truth seeking, because individuals work to maintain their own positions. Discourse serves as a context in which to engage in persuasion and conversion of others by appeals to their emotions and interests. For Laden and like-minded political philosophers, this is both a misreading of the ways in which productive political discourse proceeds and is corrosive of genuine democratic society. Laden's (2012) educational goal is to foster both the skills and supporting dispositions to generate what he refers to as a "civic virtue" of responsiveness. There is now evidence that educational programs that foster responsive transactive discourse can impact moral development and student attitudes (Nucci, Creane, & Powers (2015). What I am proposing is a process for developing a discourse orientation and skill set that would increase the likelihood of principled moral change in the social system. This is neither a conservative or liberal political agenda, because it does not presuppose the outcomes of a genuinely responsive and transactive social dialogue. What I am suggesting as an important component of character is the skill set for contributing to the sociogenetic component of the character system.

Finally, we may link this final set of skills to what William Damon and Anne Colby (Damon, 2009) have referred to as "purpose." Purpose as described by these researchers is the establishment of a set of personal goals that provide meaning and direction to a person's life. Purpose within the context of character links these personal goals to the contribution to social justice and the welfare of others. Purpose conjoined with the skills for responsive engagement would address the long sought for postconventional component of moral development and character education.

CONCLUSIONS AND FINAL THOUGHTS

Character is not a collection of virtues, personality traits, or reducible to identity, but a system that enables the person to engage the social world as a moral agent. Character does not exist as an entity because it functions coactively within the social context. As an autopoeic system character provides coherence to moral action, but not complete consistency. The lack of consistency is not a sign of moral failing or weakness of character, but the normative and expected adjustments to the social context by a functioning moral agent (Turiel, 2015). Thus, attempts to impose an impossible level of consistency through theoretical constructs such as "will" or moral identity mistakenly assume a decontextualized psychological system that has little to do with an actual human being. Similarly, theoretical critiques of character as a meaningful psychological construct because of the evidence of inconsistency (Kohlberg & Turiel, 1971) are valid only when directed at definitions of character as a set of traits, or features of personality that operate independent of the context.

In the present analysis there are four components of the character system. Three of these components comprise character as it usually thought of, and what has been referred to here as basic moral wellness. These are: (1) moral reasoning and associated domains (morality, convention, personal); (2) other regarding social emotional capacities (empathy, and emotional skills such as emotion recognition, theory of mind); (3) self regarding social emotional capacities (agency, autonomy, executive function, self-regulation). The fourth component is offered to account for a view of mature moral character that is more than compliance with the existing socially defined moral code. This would be "postconventional" character (responsive engagement and discourse skills, purpose).

As researchers we may study, measure or investigate the components of character as independent objects of study. However, the core of character is morality defined in terms of fairness and human welfare. Thus, it is an error to elevate research on any particular expression of morality, such as gratitude or compassionate love, as having particular relevance in the absence of its role or position within the character system. Because psychology is a science with competing and diverging paradigms, the study of moral reasoning and character should be broadly enough defined as to include researchers who operate within a range of research traditions.

Character is not reducible to emotional development or the development of skills associated with emotion recognition or emotion regulation. Thus the research on SEL and related educational programs is a component of character and character education, but does not encompass or include character within its definition. Research on character has largely been the search for an account of individual differences. Thus there has been an effort to try and measure character as a matter of degree— most recently the grit scale (Duckworth, 2016) has been misapplied in this way. It is unclear what benefit would come from efforts to generate these kinds of assessments. Moreover, defining character as a matter of degree misunderstands the developmental dimension of social and emotional growth and moral reasoning. Appropriate assessments would examine the forms of moral reasoning, for example, and not simply whether the person was strong in character or weak.

A more meaningful and educationally appropriate approach would be to examine all components within the character system the way that one would conduct a comprehensive physical exam, or the ways in which a pediatrician might exam a child's physical development. This would entail separate assessments for SEL competencies, moral reasoning, and moral mental health. However, even these assessments would be snapshots of disconnected components, rather than a contextualized picture.

One promising avenue would be to combine questionnaire, interview, and observational methods with the use of narrative and narrative analysis (Mclean & Syed, 2015; Pasupathi & Wainryb, 2010). Narrative analysis is particularly appealing as moral choices are impacted by the entire prior history of that person acting as a moral agent. Each moral choice both reflects and alters that history and that aspect of "self." What may appear from the outside as inconsistency in moral judgment and action (and a lack of character) may be sensible from the vantage point of the actor. Coherence rather than consistency may be found within a person's moral choices and actions by understanding the particular life-world and contextualized moral judgments as narrated by the actor (Pasupathi & Wainryb, 2010; Sarbin, 1986). One might envision a future version of a narrative assessment that could be written or oral depending upon the age and educational level of the respondent that could generate a series of scores for SEL competencies, moral reasoning (including cross-domain coordination) and purpose that might afford some access to the respondent's character system. Whether large-scale analysis of such scores would allow for the generation of a common underlying factor for character as recently proposed by Lerner and Calina (2014) is unclear. At present narrative analysis is time-consuming and expensive. However, advances in automated coding of text and voice material is making cost-effective analysis a probability. Similar forms of automated coding could be applied to assess individual's capacities for responsive engagement in sociomoral discourse. This is an avenue of research being proposed by researchers working with Anthony Laden (Levine, Shaffer, &

Nucci). All of this presupposes knowledge of moral development and contextualized moral functioning that is far from being a settled matter (Killen & Smetana, 2014).

REFERENCES

Annas, J. (2011). Practical expertise. In J. Bengson & M. A. Moffett (Eds.), *Knowing how* (pp. 101–112). Oxford, England: Oxford University Press.

Berkowitz, M. W. (2012). Moral and character education. In K. R. Harris, S. Graham, & T. Urdan (Eds.), *APA educational psychology handbook. Vol. 2: Individual differences, cultural variations, and contextual factors in educational psychology* (pp. 247–264). Washington, DC: American Psychological Association.

Berkowitz, M., & Bier, M. (2014). Research-based fundamentals of the effective promotion of character development in schools. In L. Nucci, D. Narvaez, & T. Krettenauer (Eds.). *Handbook of moral and character education* (2nd ed., pp. 248–260). New York, NY: Routledge.

Blasi, A. (2005). Moral character: A psychological approach. In D. K. Lapsley & F. C. Power (Eds.), *Character psychology and character education* (pp. 18–35). Notre Dame, IN: University of Notre Dame Press.

Blum, L. (2013). Political identity and moral education: A response to Jonathan Haidt's The Righteous Mind. *Journal of Moral Education, 42*(3), 298–315.

Carr, D. (2208). Character education and the cultivation of virtue. In L. Nucci & D. Narvaez (Eds.), *Handbook of moral and character education* (pp. 99–116). New York, NY: Routledge.

Curzer, H. (2018). Healing character flaws. In T. Harrison & D. Walker (Eds.), *Teeny tiny bits of virtue* (pp. 19–31). New York, NY: Routledge.

Damon, W. (2009). *The path to purpose: How young people find their calling in life.* New York: Simon & Schuster.

Damon, W., & Colby, A. (2015). *The power of ideals: The real story of moral choice.* New York, NY: Oxford University Press.

Davidson, M., Lickona, T., & Khmelkov, V. (2008). Smart & good schools: A new paradigm for high school character education. In L. Nucci & D. Narvaez (Eds.), *Handbook of moral and character education* (pp. 370–390). New York, NY: Routledge.

Deci, E. L., & Ryan, R. M. (2014). The importance of autonomy for development and well-being. In B. W. Sokol, F. M. Grouzet, & U. Müller (Eds.), *Self-regulation and autonomy* (pp. 19–46). New York, NY: Cambridge University Press.

Duckworth, A. (2016). *Grit: The power of passion and perseverance.* New York, NY: Simon & Schuster.

Eisenberg, N., Guthrie, I. K., Cumberland, A., Murphy, B. C., Shepard, S. A., Zhou, Q., et al. (2002). Prosocial development in early adulthood. *Journal of Personality and Social Psychology, 82,* 993–1006.

Elias, M. J., Parker, S. J., Kash, V. M.,Weissberg, R. P., & O'Brien, M. U. (2008). Social and emotional learning, moral education, and character education: A comparative analysis and a view toward convergence. In L. P. Nucci & D. Narvaez (Eds.), *Handbook of moral and character education* (pp. 248–266). New York, NY: Routledge.

Gibbs, J. C. (2013). *Moral development and reality: Beyond the theories of Kohlberg, Hoffman, and Haidt.* New York, NY: Oxford University Press.

Habermas, J., Lenhardt, C., & Nicholsen, S. W. (1991). *Moral consciousness and communicative action.* Cambridge, MA: The MIT Press.

Haidt, J. (2001). The emotional dog and its rational tail: A social intuitionist approach to moral judgment. *Psychological Review, 108,* 814–834. doi:10.1037/0033-295X.108.4.814

Haidt, J. (2012). *The righteous mind: Why good people are divided by politics and religion.* New York, NY: Vintage.

Hardy, S., & Carlo, G. (2005). Identity as a source of moral motivation. *Human Development, 48,* 232–256. doi:10.1159/000086859

Hartshorne, H., & May, M. A. (1928). *Studies in deceit.* New York, NY: Macmillan.

Jacobson, D. (2012). Moral dumbfounding and moral stupefaction. *Oxford Studies in Normative Ethics.* New York, NY: Oxford University Press.

Kerr, A., & Zelazo, P. D. (2004). Development of "hot" executive function: The children's gambling task. *Brain and Cognition, 55*(1), 148–157.

Killen, M., & J. Smetana, J. G. (Eds.), *Handbook of moral development* (2nd ed.). New York, NY: Psychology Press.

King, M. L., Carson, C., & Carson, S. (2007). *The Papers of Martin Luther King, Jr: Advocate of the social gospel, September 1948–March*

1963 (Vol. 6). Berkeley, CA: University of California Press.

Kohlberg, L. (1984). *Essays on moral development. Vol. 2: The psychology of moral development.* San Francisco, CA: Harper and Row.

Kohlberg, L., & Mayer, R. (1972). Development as the aim of education. *Harvard Educational Review, 42*(4), 449–496.

Kohlberg, L., & Turiel, E. (1971). Moral development and moral education. In G. Lesser (Ed.), *Psychology and educational practice.* Chicago, IL: Scott Foresman.

Krettenauer, T., & Hertz, S. (2015). What develops in moral identities? A critical review. *Human Development, 58,* 137–153.

Laden, A. (2012). *Reasoning: A social picture.* Oxford, England: Oxford University Press.

Lapsley. D. (1996). *Moral psychology.* Bolder, CO: Westview.

Lapsley, D. (2016). Moral self-identity and the social-cognitive theory of virtue In J. Annas, D. Narvaez, & N. E. Snow (Eds.), *Developing the virtues: Integrating perspectives* (pp. 34–68). New York, NY: Oxford University Press.

Lapsley, D., & Stey, P. (2014). Moral self-identity as the aim of education. In L. Nucci, D. Narvaez, & T. Krettenauer (Eds.). *Handbook of moral and character education* (2nd ed., pp. 84–100). New York, NY: Routledge.

Lerner, R. M. (2006). Developmental science, developmental systems, and contemporary theories of human development. In W. Damon & R. M. Lerner (Eds.), *Handbook of Child psychology: Vol. 1. Theoretical models of human development* (6th ed., pp. 1–17). Hoboken, NJ: Wiley.

Lerner, R., & Callina, K. (2014). The study of character development: Towards tests of a relational developmental systems model. *Human Development, 57*(6), 322–346. doi:10.1159/000368784

Martin, J., Sokol, B., & Elfers, T. (2008). Taking and coordinating perspectives: From prereflective interactivity, through reflective intersubjectivity, to metareflective sociality. *Human Development, 51,* 294–317.

McGrath, R. E. (2016, July). *Essential virtues.* Presented at the Workshop on Approaches to the Development of Character, National Academy of Sciences, Washington, DC.

McLean, K. C., & Syed, M. (2015). Personal, master, and alternative narratives: An integrative framework for understanding identity development in context. *Human Development, 58,* 318–359.

Miller, J. G., & Bland, C. (2014). A cultural psychology perspective on moral development. In M. Killen & J. G. Smetana (Eds.), *Handbook of moral development* (2nd ed., pp. 299–314). New York, NY: Taylor & Francis.

Narvaez, D., & Lapsley, D. (2005). The psychological foundations of everyday morality and moral expertise. In D. Lapsley & C. Power (Eds.), *Character psychology and character education* (pp. 140–165). Notre Dame: IN: University of Notre Dame Press

Nucci, L. P. (2001). *Education in the moral domain.* Cambridge, England: Cambridge University Press.

Nucci, L. (2004). Reflections on the moral self construct. In D. K. Lapsley & D. Narvaez (Eds.), *Moral development, self and identity* (pp. 111–132). Mahwah, NJ: Erlbaum.

Nucci, L. (2014). The personal and the moral. In M. Killen & J. G. Smetana (Eds.), *Handbook of moral development* (2nd ed., pp. 538–558). New York, NY: Taylor & Francis. doi:10.4324/9780203581957.ch25

Nucci, L. (2015, October). Recovering the role of reasoning in moral education. Keynote address at the annual meeting of the Association for Moral Education, Santos, Brazil.

Nucci, L., Creane, M., & Powers, D. W. (2015). Integrating moral and social development within middle school social studies: A social cognitive domain approach. *Journal of Moral Education. 44,* 479–496. doi: 10.1080/03057240.2015.1087391

Nucci, L., Turiel, E., & Roded, A. D. (2017). Continuities and discontinuities in the development of moral judgments. *Human Development, 60.*

Overton, W. F. (2015). Process and relational developmental systems. In W. F. Overton & P. C. Molenaar (Eds.), *Handbook of child psychology and developmental science: Vol. 1. Theory and method* (7th ed.). Hoboken, NJ: Wiley.

Pasupathi, M., & Wainryb, C. (2010). Developing moral agency through narrative. *Human Development, 53,* 55–80. doi:10.1159/000288208

Piaget, J. (1985). *The equilibration of cognitive structures.* Chicago, IL: University of Chicago Press.

Proulx, T., & Chandler, M. J. (2009). Jekyll and Hyde and me: Age-graded differences in conceptions of self-unity. *Human development, 52*(5), 261–286.

Rawls, J. (2001). *Justice as fairness: A restatement.* Cambridge, MA: Harvard University Press.

Recchia, H., Wainryb, C., Bourne, S., & Pasupathi, M. (2015). Children's and adolescents' accounts of helping and hurting: Lessons about the development of moral agency. *Child Development, 86*, 864–876. doi:10.1111/cdev.12349.

Richardson, C. B., Mulvey, K. L., & Killen, M. (2012). Extending social domain theory with a process-based account of moral judgments. *Human Development, 55*(1), 4–25.

Saarni, C. (1997). Emotional competence and self-regulation in childhood. In P. Salovey & D. J. Sluyter (Eds.), *Emotional development and emotional intelligence: Educational implications* (pp. 35–66). New York, NY: Basic Books.

Saarni, C. (2007). The development of emotional competence: Pathways for helping children to become emotionally intelligent. In R. Bar-On, J. G. Maree, & M. J. Elias (Eds.), *Educating people to be emotionally intelligent* (pp. 15–36). Westport, CT: Praeger.

Sarbin, T. R. (Ed.). (1986). The narrative as a root metaphor for psychology. In *Narrative psychology: The storied nature of human conduct* (pp. 3–21). New York, NY: Praeger.

Saxe, G. B., & Esmonde, I. (2012). *Cultural development of mathematical ideas: Papua New Guinea studies*. New York, NY: Cambridge University Press.

Smetana, J. G. (2010). *Adolescents, families, and social development: How teens construct their worlds*. New York, NY: John Wiley & Sons.

Smetana, J., Jambon, M., & Ball, C. (2014). The social domain approach to children's moral and social judgments. In M. Killen & J. Smetana (Eds.), *Handbook of moral development* (2nd ed., pp. 23–45). New York, NY: Psychology Press. doi:10.4324/9780203581957.ch2

Sokol, B. W., Hammond, S. I., & Berkowitz, M. W. (2010). The developmental contours of character. In T. Lovat, R. Toomey, & N. Clement (Eds.), *International research handbook on values education and student wellbeing* (pp. 579–603). Dordrecht, Netherlands: Springer. doi:10.1007/978-90-481-8675-4

Thompson, R. (2014). Conscience development in early childhood. In M. Killen & J. Smetana (Eds.), *Handbook of moral development* (2nd ed., pp. 73–92). New York, NY: Psychology Press.

Turiel, E. (1983). *The development of social knowledge: Morality and convention*. Cambridge England: Cambridge University Press.

Turiel, E. (2002). *The culture of morality: Social development, context, and conflict*. Cambridge: England: Cambridge University Press.

Turiel, E. (2010). Snap judgment? Not so fast: Thought, reasoning, and choice as psychological realities. *Human Development, 53*(3), 105–109.

Turiel, E. (2015). Moral development. In W. Overton & R. Molenaar (Eds.), *Handbook of child psychology and developmental science, theory and method* (Vol. 1). New York, NY: Wiley

Turiel, E., & Nucci, L. (2018). Moral development in context. In A. Dick & U. Mueller (Eds.) *Advancing developmental science: Philosophy, theory, and method*. New York, NY: Psychology Press.

Wainryb, C. (2011). "And so they ordered me to kill a person": Conceptualizing the impacts of child soldiering on the development of moral agency. *Human Development, 54*, 273–300. doi:10.1159/000331482

Wainryb, C., & Pasupathi, M. (2015). Saints, and the rest of us: Broadening the perspective on moral identity development. *Human Development, 58*(3), 154–163.

Witherington, D. C. (2011). Taking emergence seriously: The centrality of circular causality for dynamic systems approaches to development. *Human Development, 54*(2), 66–92.

Wolf, S. (1982). Moral saints. *The Journal of Philosophy, 79*, 419–439.

Zelazo, P. D., Mueller, U., Douglas, F., & Marcovitch, S. (2003). The development of executive function in early childhood. *Monographs for the Society of Research in Child Development, 68*, 1–137.

ON THE IMPORTANCE OF COHERENCE IN THE STUDY OF CHARACTER DEVELOPMENT

Kristina Schmid Callina and Richard M. Lerner
Tufts University

Nucci (this issue) gives a compelling conceptualization of the ideas needed to understand character as a multifaceted developmental system. In this article, we focus on the idea of coherence as it applies to understanding character development, education, and assessment. Using ideas from relational developmental systems (RDS) metatheory, we rationalize the fundamental significance of coherence for studying character virtues. We propose that coherence may be understood in at least 3 interrelated ways: as the appropriate application of morality to a particular situation; as employing the right virtue, in the right amount, at the right time (Aristotle's concept of *phronesis*); and as an integrated system of moral concepts. To test these ideas, we point to the need for innovations in developmental methodology and collaborative science that we hope will mark the future of RDS-based studies of positive character development.

Character is a multifaceted system. Nucci (this issue) gives a compelling conceptualization of the ideas needed to understand this system. His article provides a framework that brings much-needed integration to the field of character development and education. This integration is necessary to reconcile diverse viewpoints and definitions of character, and may enable practitioners, researchers, educators, parents, and mentors to move forward with confidence in educating and assessing character development. Therefore, we are tempted to provide only a concise but accurate statement in response to his article: We agree!

In particular, we agree with the relational development systems-based approach to char-

acter development taken by Nucci. In this article we will offer some ideas that serve to complement Nucci's article. Specifically, we will expand on his assertion that "any account of character has to look at coherence and not consistency." We will further argue that coherence is fundamental to the study of the character system and fundamental to enhancing character education.

THEORETICAL PERSPECTIVES FOR UNDERSTANDING CHARACTER DEVELOPMENT

As described by Lerner, Callina, Nucci, and others (Callina, Ryan, et al., 2017; Lerner &

• **Correspondence concerning this article should be addressed to:** Kristina Schmid Callina, kristina.callina@tufts.edu

ISSN 1543-1223

Callina, 2014; Nucci, this issue), character development may be usefully understood within the frame of relational development systems (RDS) metatheory. RDS represents a set of concepts about human development which emphasize that developmental outcomes—an individual's character attributes, for example—depend on the ongoing coactions between the individual and his or her context (Overton, 2015). Bronfenbrenner's bioecological systems model (Bronfenbrenner & Morris, 2006) is a well-known example of a model framed by RDS metatheory (e.g., see Lerner, 2017, and Lerner, Vandell, & Tirrell, this issue, for a discussion of this link). The contexts included in the bioecological model contain many levels of the ecology: the natural or built environment; relationships with other people, including caregivers, teachers, neighbors, et cetera.; societal influences and institutions; and culture. The essential feature of Bronfenbrenner's model (often represented by concentric circles, with the person at the center and the "macro" developmental influences at the outside; Bronfenbrenner, 1979) is the bidirectional arrows that mark the mutually influential relations within and across all levels of organization within the ecology.

RDS in Overview

As described by Overton (2015), RDS metatheory is derived from a process-relational paradigm, as compared to a Cartesian worldview (e.g., involving mind/body dualism and other split conceptions) that has framed ontology for much of human history. The process-relational paradigm focuses on process (systematic changes in the developmental system), holism (the meanings of entities and events derive from the context in which they are embedded), relational analysis (assessment of the mutually influential relations within the developmental system), and the use of multiple perspectives and explanatory forms (employment of ideas from multiple theory-based models of change within and of the developmental system). Within the process-relational paradigm, the organism is seen as inherently active, self-creating (autopoietic), self-organizing, self-regulating (agentic), nonlinear and complex, and adaptive (Overton, 2015). As such, researchers who subscribe to RDS metatheory use models of development that emphasize the integration of different levels of organization, ranging from biology and physiology to culture and history (e.g., Gottlieb, 1998, 2004; Mascolo & Fischer, 2015; Mistry & Dutta, 2015). Thus, the conceptual emphasis in RDS theories is placed on mutually influential relations between individuals and contexts, represented as individual ⇔ context relations.

The bidirectional arrow used in the RDS representation of person ⇔ context relations is intended to emphasize that the coaction of individual and context involves the entire developmental system. As such, the relations among levels of the autopoietic system, and not independent linear combinatorial attributes, are the focus in such a model. Indeed, the fusion of individual and context within the developmental system means that any portion of the system is inextricably embedded with—or embodied by, in Overton's (2015) terms—all other portions of the developmental system. Embodiment refers to the way individuals behave, experience, and live in the world by their being active agents with particular kinds of bodies; the body is integratively understood as form (a biological referent), as lived experience (a psychological referent), and as an entity in active engagement with the world (a sociocultural and historical referent; Overton, 2015).

The embeddedness within history (temporality) is of fundamental significance in RDS theories (Elder, Shanahan, & Jennings, 2015). Embeddedness means that change is constant in the developmental system. There may be either random or systematic changes in person ⇔ context relations across time and place (Elder et al., 2015). Bronfenbrenner referred to temporality as the *chronosystem* in his process-person ⇔ context-time model of individual ⇔ context relations (Bronfenbrenner &

Morris, 2006). The presence of such temporality in the developmental system means that there always exists some potential for systematic change, for plasticity, in the relational developmental system.

This point is a crucial component of RDS thinking; it is the component of RDS that gives it power to influence practice and policy across any domain of human flourishing. There always exists the potential for (relative) plasticity in human development (Gottlieb, 1998, 2004; Lerner, 2010). Adjustments to any level of the ecology, from improvements in nutrition to more equitable social policies, may alter the course of an individual's embodied person ⇔ context relations. Accordingly, individual developmental trajectories are marked by plasticity.

Developmental trajectories are plastic and diverse, but not infinitely so; constraints imposed by the context channel pathways of goal selection and attainment (Nurmi, 2004). Developmental pathways are not completely random, either; the individual has agency to guide his or her relations with the context. When individual ⇔ context relations are mutually beneficial—that is, when both individual and context engage in positive or healthy exchanges—these relations are termed adaptive developmental relations (Brandtstädter, 1998). In order for the person to maintain such adaptive developmental regulations with the context, the individual must enact specific behaviors at specific times in life and in specific settings. In other words, the individual must be flexible and adaptive in order to maintain positive individual ⇔ context relations in the complex and changing ecology of human development. Thus, we argue that adaptive development is marked by coherence of the underlying structures that promote mutually beneficial person ⇔ context relations, and not by consistency of functioning. We elaborate on these ideas and their importance for studying character development below.

In an RDS-based approach to understanding development, neither an individual's attributes nor the context alone can explain how development proceeds in any particular instance; the individual and the context are entirely integrated. Therefore, any explanation of development must involve understanding the person, the context, and how they relate to one another across time and place (Elder et al., 2015). RDS theories are therefore useful for understanding any developmental phenomena, including moral character and character virtue development.

An RDS-Based Conception of Character Development

Lerner and Callina (2014) presented an RDS approach to studying character development (see too Callina, Ryan et al., 2017; Nucci, this issue). According to this approach, character develops through "a specific set of mutually beneficial relations that vary across time and … place, between person and context … and, in particular, between the individual and other individuals that comprise his or her context" (Lerner & Callina, 2014, p. 323). In other words, character constitutes attributes of an individual's relations with his or her social context that involve coherently "doing the right thing" (morally and behaviorally) to provide mutually positive benefits to both self and others. As we will suggest in greater detail in this article, coherence of the character system—and not consistency across time and place—is the hallmark of character virtue development (Lerner & Callina, 2014; Nucci, this issue).

The importance for human flourishing of mutually beneficial relations between an individual and his or her community context is widely accepted among scholars who study character development and education. For example, Nucci (2001) emphasized that character virtue development involves "human welfare, justice and rights, which are a function of inherent features of interpersonal relations" (p. 7), and Berkowitz (2012) described character as "a public system of universal concerns about human welfare, justice, and rights that all rational people would want others to adhere to" (p. 249). Narvaez (2008), highlighting the contextual, adaptive nature of character, explained that a person with character lives a life that is good for one to live *within one's community*.

In short, from an RDS-based perspective, character involves a person's positive and adaptive actions-in-context. Thus, to understand character development, researchers, practitioners, and educators must seek to understand the underlying structure of character that allows a person to direct the course of adaptive regulations with the environment. Nucci (this issue) proposes that this structure is comprised of several components: moral cognition, moral agency, and moral enactment or performance. A fourth component of character, which Nucci describes as an orientation to principled moral change, involves acting positively on the social world (one's family, school, or community, for instance) to promote thriving within the developmental system (Lerner, 2017).

Taken together, these four components can be used to identify individuals with "good character." Researchers often turn to assessments of character virtues, such as honesty, humility, empathy, or hope to describe good character and to evaluate character promotion programs. Nucci (this issue) is somewhat critical of this approach, insofar as virtue research attempts to identify a universal, acontextual set of character attributes that all people should have or ignores the central role of morality in the character system. We agree with Nucci's critiques of virtue research, but would nevertheless suggest that character virtues play a supporting role in moral cognitions (associated character virtues include intellectual humility, curiosity, etc.), moral agency (e.g., empathy and other socioemotional skills), the enactment of moral character (e.g., self-regulation and executive functioning), and moral change (e.g., leadership, generosity, etc.). Moreover, character virtues can be taught, assessed, and used to guide curriculum development. Recall that an RDS approach to character virtue development prioritizes mutually beneficial

person ⇔ context (and person ⇔ person) relations (Lerner & Callina, 2014). We see the individual's contribution to these relations as necessarily moral, that is, as promoting the welfare and rights of others within a community. Accordingly, from an RDS perspective character virtues support the moral core that is the essential feature of Nucci's (this issue) character system.

If, as we contend, research on character development within an RDS perspective should seek to understand coherence of functioning (i.e., doing what is needed to promote mutual benefits for person and context), rather than consistency (i.e., doing the same things no matter what is needed at a specific time and place), a focus on how character virtues support moral contributions of the individual to his or her community will be important. Character virtue research will be most useful when researchers and practitioners are sensitive to the changing nature of person ⇔ context relations across time and place; good character for a 14-year-old high school student dealing with cyber bullying in his school will look different than what one would expect from a 28-year-old military officer seeking to promote discipline and cohesion within her unit.

THE IMPORTANCE OF COHERENCE FOR UNDERSTANDING CHARACTER DEVELOPMENT

Nucci (this issue) defines coherence as it relates to character development as "the rational connection among contextualized moral judgments and actions as seen from the vantage point of the actor rather than the similarity in actions within a given type of situation as seen from the point of view of an observer" (p. 15). From this conception of coherence, the construct is part of the phenomenology of the actor (e.g., see Spencer, Swanson, & Harpalani, 2015). We would add that character development researchers and character educators can also appraise (observe) coherence, as compared to consistency. Indeed, within an RDS model, we may hypothesize that adaptive relations between actors and observers would involve congruence between them in judgments about whether manifestations of character reflect coherence across time and place.

Accordingly, our expansion of Nucci's (this issue) definition proposes that coherence may be understood in at least three interrelated ways. First, coherence may be thought of as a system of integrated moral concepts. Different facets of moral functioning must be in a person's repertoire in order for him or her to act coherently as compared to consistently. Second, borrowing from Aristotle's concept of *phronesis* (*The Nicomachean Ethics*, 1985), developmental scientists may look for coherence of the moral core in the application of a specific character virtue to maintain the adaptive functioning of a specific individual in a specific context (Bornstein, 2017). Third, as Nucci (this issue) and others (Smetana, Jambon, & Ball, 2014) have argued, morality is not the primary motivation for all behavior, and so coherence may be thought of as the appropriate application of morality to a particular situation. It is useful to discuss these three ideas in more detail.

Coherence may refer to the extent to which the components of the character system are integrated or synchronized (Nucci, this issue; Turiel, 2015): these structures are moral cognitions, agency, enactment, and change. Researchers and practitioners should search for evidence of positive character not in the consistent application of virtues across domains and over time, but rather in the adaptive development of the four character components outlined by Nucci: moral cognition, moral mental health, moral enactment, and an orientation to principled moral change.

Throughout the course of human development, developmental scientists should not impose an unreasonable expectation of consistency in moral behaviors, or attribute lack of consistency to moral failing. There are two reasons for this view. First, as Turiel (2015) notes, "alternative acts seemingly different

from each other ... can be motivated by similar moral concepts" (p. 504). Second, developmental scientists have to allow for mistakes in the course of "the normative and expected adjustments to the social context by a functioning moral agent" (Nucci, this issue, p. 12). RDS concepts justify a hopeful orientation to human development; owing to the potential for plasticity, every individual can be placed on a pathway marked by positive character development. We subscribe to a positive development approach to promoting character, which suggests that every individual has strengths that can be leveraged (by practitioners, educators, parents, mentors, etc.) to enhance character virtue development (Callina, Mueller, Napolitano, Lerner, & Lerner, 2016).

Different virtues may be expressed in different amounts, in different contexts, at different times, which points to Aristotle's concept of phronesis (*The Nicomachean Ethics*, 1985). Phronesis, also referred to as "practical wisdom," allows an individual to find the right balance of a given virtue, so as to avoid vice on the one hand or zealotry on the other. Applying this concept to modern theories of positive, adaptive psychosocial functioning, Seligman (2015) argues that psychological health relies on the presence of strengths (virtues) and is threatened by "the absence, the excess, or the opposite of strengths" (p. 4). Questions about coherence versus consistency of character with respect to variation in context may be especially useful for understanding the developmental course of character among diverse individuals (Lerner & Callina, 2014).

For instance, are particular indicators of character, such as generosity, manifested consistently across time and place? Research suggests that they are not (Nucci & Turiel, 2009). Alternatively, does the idea of coherence (as contrasted with consistency) mark a person's character across time and place? We believe that affirmative answers to this question suggest a promising area of inquiry for the burgeoning science of character virtue development. Rather than a concern about merely increasing scores on a measure of character, such as grit, researchers and practitioners should seek to understand whether a person applies task "stick-to-itiveness" in some circumstances, but employs ingenuity—and thus the generation of potentially different actions—in the face of an intractable problem.

IMPLICATIONS OF COHERENCE AND RDS FOR STUDYING CHARACTER DEVELOPMENT

The focus on coherence for future research in character development presents challenges for scholars. Much of the prior research on character has focused on assessing individual and group differences in the levels of a particular character virtue and on increasing it (Lerner & Callina, 2014; Nucci, this issue). Not surprisingly, Nucci (this issue) envisions a comprehensive assessment of character that attends to each of the four character components. These assessments must, in turn, be contextualized. A holistic approach to studying character would therefore involve the use of multiple methods (e.g., qualitative and quantitative), multiple informants and/or observational data, and longitudinal data to model change. One example of character virtue development research framed by RDS metatheory is the ongoing study of character and leadership at the U.S. Military Academy at West Point, called Project Arete (Callina, Ryan et al., 2017; Matthews, 2016). We hope that the findings from Project Arete and other studies will demonstrate the utility of applying the concept of coherence to understanding character development in specific contexts, especially educational and out-of-school time activities (see Callina et al., 2016, for more examples of RDS-based character virtue development research).

Advances in methodological and data analytic tools will also be required to understand coherence in character development. Researchers should attempt to design studies that are person-centered, rather than based on group averages (Rose, 206). RDS meta-theory emphasizes the nonergodicity of human development (e.g., Mascolo & Fischer, 2015; Mole-

naar & Nesselroade, 2015; Raeff, 2016). Nonergodicity refers to statistical methods that provide information about individuals' dynamic and diverse developmental trajectories (Molenaar & Nesselroade, 2015; Rose, 2016). In other words, character development research—including character education program evaluation—should strive to model pathways of development, development across different contexts, and the within- and between-person diversity in the ways in which character attributes are expressed (e.g., Molenaar & Nesselroade, 2015; Rose, 2016). In addition to the technological advances that Nucci (this issue) proposes to analyze large amounts of qualitative data (e.g., automated text coding), we believe that methodological innovations such as integrative data analysis (Curran & Hussong, 2009; Callina, Johnson et al., 2017) may promote the large-scale data analysis procedures necessary to use to understand coherence.

Taken together, our recommendations for the future study of character development will require the kind of collaborative science that is more commonly seen in biology, chemistry, and physics: networks of researchers seeking to integrate multiple sources of data and working to translate findings from the lab to the classroom. Such advances in scholarship would serve not only the science of character virtues development. The attendees of the July, 2016 National Academy of Sciences meeting, from which this article and the special issue within which it appears were derived, included researchers, policymakers, practitioners, and educators from both out-of-school-time and school-based programs. We believe that our vision for the future of character virtue development research will promote understanding across these stakeholder groups of the diverse ways in which individuals coherently engage in mutually beneficial relations with their context.

CONCLUSIONS

We believe that developmental models of character must focus on coherence of character across time and place. Indeed, as Nucci (this issue) emphasizes, attempts to impose an impossible level of consistency on the conceptualization or operationalization of character mistakenly assume a decontextualized psychological system that has little to do with an actual human being. However, if there is no average individual (Rose, 2016), and if positive and adaptive character development varies across time and place, how do educators provide the experiences essential to develop each person in their charge into an individual of good character?

We believe that a new approach to evidence-based practice in character education is needed. This approach might be usefully framed by the specificity principle (Bornstein, 2017) that indicates the multiple dimensions of individual and context that must be integrated in research to enable character educators to educate youth with the capacity of manifest coherence. For instance, such integration may elucidate what specific character virtues, for individuals of what specific ages and other specific demographic attributes, developing in what specific settings, and having what specific experiences (e.g., participating, or not, in specific youth-development and/or character-education programs), and linked to what other specific individual and ecological variables, result in what specific developmental trajectories of both character virtues development and other theoretically specified features of human development (e.g., active and positive civic engagement; Lerner, 2017) across what specific portions of the life course.

Addressing these questions of coherence in character requires coherence among character researchers. We believe that such coherence in scholarship is possible, if the above-noted innovations in conceptualization of character development, developmental methodology, and collaborative science mark the future of RDS-based studies of character. Empowered with answers to the set of questions involved in framing research through the specificity principle, practitioners, educators, and policymakers may then be able to design and enact the nuanced programs that will embrace the diversity of each individual and set him or her on a thriving trajectory marked by the development of positive character.

Acknowledgment: The preparation of this article was supported in part by a grant from the Templeton Religion Trust. Author's contact information: Kristina Callina, Institute for Applied Research in Youth Development, Tufts University, 26 Winthrop Street, Medford, MA 02155. Email: kristina.callina@tufts.edu.

REFERENCES

Aristotle. (1985). *Nicomachean ethics* (T. Irwin, Trans.). Indianapolis, IN: Hackett.

Berkowitz, M. W. (2012). Moral and character education. In K. R. Harris, S. Graham, & T. Urdan (Eds.), *APA educational psychology handbook. Vol. 2: Individual differences, cultural variations, and contextual factors in educational psychology* (pp. 247–264). Washington, DC: American Psychological Association.

Bornstein, M. H. (2017). The specificity principle in acculturation science. *Perspectives in Psychological Science, 12*(1), 3–45.

Bronfenbrenner, U. (1979). *The ecology of human development: Experiments by design and nature.* Cambridge, MA: Harvard University.

Brandtstädter, J. (1998). Action perspectives on human development. In R. M. Lerner (Ed.), *Handbook of child psychology* (Vol. 1, 5th ed., pp. 807–866). New York, NY: Wiley.

Bronfenbrenner, U., & Morris, P. A. (2006). The bioecological model of human development. In R. M. Lerner (Ed.). *Handbook of child psychology. Vol. 1: Theoretical models of human development* (6th ed., pp. 795–828). Hoboken, NJ: Wiley.

Callina, K. S., Johnson, S. K., Tirrell, J., Batanova, M., Weiner, M., & Lerner, R. M. (2017). Modeling pathways of character development across the first three decades of life: An application of integrative data analysis techniques. *Journal of Youth and Adolescence, 46,* 1216–1237.

Callina, K. S., Mueller, M. K., Napolitano, C. M., Lerner, J. V., & Lerner, R. M. (2016). Positive youth development: Relational developmental systems approaches to thriving from childhood to early adulthood. In S. J. Lopez, L. M. Edwards, & S. C. Marques (Eds.), *The Oxford handbook of positive psychology* (3rd ed.). New York, NY: Oxford University Press. doi:10.1093/oxfordhb/9780199396511.013.11

Callina, K. S., Ryan, D., Murray, E. D., Colby, A., Damon, W., Matthews, M., & Lerner, R. M. (2017) Developing leaders of character at the United States Military Academy: A relational developmental systems analysis. *Journal of College and Character, 18*(1), 9–27.

Curran, P. J., & Hussong, A. M. (2009). Integrative data analysis: The simultaneous analysis of multiple data sets. *Psychology Methods, 14*, 81–100.

Elder, G. H., Shanahan, M. J., & Jennings, J. A. (2015). Human development in time and place. In M. H. Bornstein & T. Leventhal (Eds.), *Handbook of child psychology and developmental science. Vol. 4: Ecological settings and processes in developmental systems* (7th ed., pp. 6–54). Hoboken, NJ: Wiley.

Gottlieb, G. (1998). Normally occurring environmental and behavioral influences on gene activity: From central dogma to probabilitstic epigenesis. *Psychological Review, 105*, 792–802.

Gottlieb, G. (2004). Normally occurring environmental and behavioral influences on gene activity. In C. Garcia Coll, E. Bearer, & R. M. Lerner (Eds.). *Nature and nurture: The complex interplay of genetic and environmental influences on human behavior and development* (pp. 85–106). Mahwah, NJ: Erlbaum

Lerner, R. M. (2010). Applied developmental science: Definitions and dimensions. In V. Maholmes & C. G. Lomonaco (Eds.), *Applied research in child and adolescent development: A practical guide* (pp. 37–58). New York, NY: Taylor & Francis.

Lerner, R. M. (Editor-in-Chief). (2015). Preface. In *Handbook of child psychology and developmental science* (7th ed., pp. xv–xxi). Hoboken, NJ: Wiley.

Lerner, R. M. (2017). Character development among youth: Linking lives in time and place. *International Journal of Behavioral Development.* doi:10.1177/0165025417711057

Lerner, R. M., & Callina, K. S. (2014). Relational developmental systems theories and the ecological validity of experimental designs. *Human Development, 56*(6), 372–380.

Lerner, R. M., Vandell, D. L., & Tirrell, J. M. (2017). Approaches to the development of character. *Journal of Character Education, 13*(1), v–x.

Mascolo, M. F., & Fischer, K. W. (2015) Dynamic development of thinking, feeling, and acting. In W. F. Overton & P. C. Molenaar (Eds.), *Theory and method: Vol. 1. Handbook of child psychology and developmental science* (7th ed., pp. 113–161). Hoboken, NJ: Wiley.

Matthews, M. D. (2016, December 29). Project Arete: Understanding character and leadership at West Point. *Psychology Today.* Retrieved from https://www.psychologytoday.com/blog/head-strong/201612/project-arete

Mistry, J., & Dutta, R. (2015). Human development and culture: Conceptual and methodological Issues. In W. F. Overton & P. C. Molenaar (Eds.), *Handbook of child psychology and developmental science: Vol. 1. Theory and method* (7th ed., pp. 369–406). Hoboken, NJ: Wiley.

Molenaar, P. C. M., & Nesselroade, J. R. (2015). Systems methods for developmental research. In W. F. Overton & P. C. Molenaar (Eds.), *Handbook of child psychology and developmental science: Vol. 1. Theory and method* (7th ed., pp. 652–682). Hoboken, NJ: Wiley.

Narvaez, D. (2008). Human flourishing and moral development: Cognitive and neurobiological perspectives of virtue development. In L. Nucci & D. Narvaez (Eds.), *Handbook of moral and character education* (pp. 310–327) Oxford, England: Routledge.

Nucci, L. P., & Turiel, E. (2009) Capturing the complexity of moral development and education. *Mind, Brain, and Education, 3*, 151–159.

Nucci, L. P. (2001). *Education in the moral domain.* Cambridge, England: Cambridge University Press.

Nucci, J. E. (2017). Character: A multifaceted developmental system. *Journal of Character Education, 13*(1) 1–16.

Nurmi, J. E. (2004). Socialization and self-development: Channeling, selection, adjustment, and reflection. In R. M. Lerner & L. Steinberg (Eds.), *Handbook of adolescent psychology* (Vol. 2, pp. 85–124). Hoboken, NJ: Wiley.

Overton, W. F. (2015). Process and relational developmental systems. In W. F. Overton & P. C. Molenaar (Eds.), *Handbook of child psychology and developmental science: Vol. 1. Theory and method* (7th ed., pp. 9–62). Hoboken, NJ: Wiley.

Raeff, C. (2016). *Exploring the dynamics of human development: An integrative approach.* London, England: Oxford University Press.

Rose, T. (2015). *The end of average: How we succeed in a world that values sameness.* New York, NY: HarperCollins.

Seligman, M. E. P. (2015). Chris Peterson's unfinished masterwork: The real mental illnesses. *The Journal of Positive Psychology, 10*(1), 3–6.

Smetana, J. G., Jambon, M., & Ball, C. (2014). The social domain approach to children's moral and social judgments. In M. Killen & J. G. Smetana (eds.), *Handbook of moral development* (2nd ed., pp. 23–45).

Spencer, M. B., Swanson, D. P., & Harpalani, V. (2015). Development of the self. In M. Lamb (Ed.), *Handbook of child psychology and developmental science: Vol. 3. Social, emotional, and personality development* (7th ed., pp. 750–793). Hoboken, NJ: Wiley.

Turiel, E. (2015). Moral development. In W. F. Overton & P. C. Molenaar (Eds.), *Handbook of child psychology and developmental science: Vol. 1. Theory and method* (7th ed., pp. 484–522). Hoboken, NJ: Wiley.

☆ Character.org
Since 1993

Join Character.org today, and help us empower everyone to be their absolute best!

If you believe that good character is essential to create a more ethical and compassionate world, then you belong among Character.org's membership of character leaders.

By becoming a member, not only will you directly support Character.org's effective framework that helps create Communities of Character, you will also be making a clear statement that good character should be a priority for everyone, everywhere.

All of our members receive a host of exclusive benefits, including:
- Access to the latest and greatest resources
- An opportunity to participate in a member meeting at the National Forum
- Discounted rates and special offers on publications and events

Join today at www.character.org/donate

THE ESSENTIALS AND COMPLEXITIES OF CHARACTER
Reflections on Nucci's Multifaceted Model

Robert E. McGrath

Fairleigh Dickinson University

Larry Nucci, in his article "Character: A Multifaceted Developmental System," has outlined a model of character that focuses on 4 domains of the moral system. This response focuses on 2 issues. The first is Nucci's equation of character with moral functioning. My research has led me to propose that 3 elements are essential to any adequate theory of character, called caring, inquisitiveness, and self-control. These emerge across a number of virtue theories, as well as models of essential skills and even literary references. In particular, I suggest that inquisitiveness and self-control are indicators of character even when not used to support moral ends, so long as they are not used to support immoral ones. Second, I think the model Nucci proposes for moral character is incomplete, as it fails to outline the competing considerations that enter into moral decision-making. Character education programs should acknowledge and even emphasize how these competing considerations can lead to nonmoral decision-making when environmental factors encourage poor choices.

In his article, "Character: A Multifaceted Developmental System," Larry Nucci is attempting something that I think is very exciting. He has clearly taken to heart Kohlberg's (Kohlberg & Hersch, 1977) dismissal of character education as training in a "bag of virtues." In response, Nucci seems to be rejecting the traditional approach to thinking of character as an enumeration of attributes, such as honesty or fairness. In its place, he is attempting to reconceptualize character as a relational developmental system (Lerner & Schmid Callina, 2014) consisting of four interlocking elements. These elements operate together to generate moral judgments and actions in a manner influenced by the individual's developmental status and environmental context. Character in this framework is no longer a list, but an organization.

Why do I call this approach exciting? Historically, my research has focused on person measurement, and when I was asked to reflect

• **Correspondence concerning this article should be addressed to:** Robert E. McGrath, mcgrath@fdu.edu

on Nucci's article, it was to be from the perspective of a personality researcher. In fact,
much of my work on character has focused on
its structure, some of which I will cite below.
For these reasons, I have a fondness for
research that attempts to identify "true" structure. That said, this approach can go only so far
in terms of understanding a construct so culturally shaped as character; the process by which
character affects and is affected by the person's environment very quickly emerges as a
topic of great interest.

In fact, even the field of personality
research has started to come to grips with this
issue, and it is striking to me the parallels I see
between Nucci's efforts to embed character in
the self-system and relatively recent work on
identity as a personality concept (e.g., McAdams & Manczak, 2015; McAdams & McLean,
2013). Elsewhere, I have even suggested that
one of the central features distinguishing character education from other forms of education
for personal growth is the focus on identity, on
"who will I be?" rather than "what will I do?"
(McGrath, 2017). I see a potentially fruitful
marriage across research traditions, in which
methodologies developed for purposes of
uncovering an individual's narrative identity
are applied to moral identity as well.

Despite my enthusiasm for the potential of
this approach, the remainder of this article will
be devoted to two concerns about the model
Nucci presents. First, there is another lesson
from personality research to be learned that I
think will enrich the model he is presenting.
Personality researchers have been attempting
to integrate their traditional taxonomic
approach to understanding personality as a
series of dimensions with the new perspective
on narrative identity (McAdams & Pals, 2006),
though it can be questioned how successful
those efforts have been. I think it will be similarly important to consider structural work on
character, to see what implications it might
have for the model he is sculpting. In particular, my work leads me to suspect Nucci has
omitted at least one essential component of

character, one that requires looking further
beyond the moral agent.

Second, morality is a very complicated relational developmental system. I fear the four
units Nucci describes as underlying moral
character does not come close to capturing the
complexity of that system. That is, perhaps he
also needs to look more closely within the
moral agent.

THE ESSENTIALS OF CHARACTER

Nucci's equation of character with morality
has a rich heritage among experts in character
education (e.g., Berkowitz, Althof, & Bier,
2012), but there are alternative perspectives. In
particular, the first lengthy discussion in
recorded history of what we now would think
of as character, Aristotle's *Nicomachean Ethics*, considered it to have both moral and intellectual elements (Bartlett & Collins, 2007),
while Lickona and Davidson (2005) focused
on moral and productive elements. Is character
simply what we decide it is in any time or
place, or is there an essential element to its
nature?

There are at least three reasons the answer
to this question can be important. First, if character is just a cultural construct, there may be
no adequate defense against Kohlberg's "bag
of virtues" objection to character education.
Second, character education can be reduced to
convincing people to comply with social convention. Third, a purely socially constructed
list of the elements of character can expand
indefinitely.

One possible solution to this problem
would simply declare Aristotle and others
wrong and Nucci right, and reduce character to
the moral. Recently, I suggested an alternative
(yes, admittedly structural) solution. I suggested three key elements of character, or key
virtues, consist of caring, inquisitiveness, and
self-control (McGrath, 2015). My colleagues
and I have recently completed a follow-up
analysis of this model (McGrath, Greenberg,
& Hall-Simmonds, in press) that replicated

this model across 12 samples from around the world. These samples completed several different measures of character, in different languages, and data were analyzed using several different statistical methods. I should make it clear there are real limitations to the research underlying this model. The studies used data reflecting only one model of character, though this model is particularly popular and comprehensive (Peterson & Seligman, 2004). The samples were largely Western or at least highly educated. Finally, the model was derived largely from cross-sectional self-report data, data sources Nucci justifiably criticizes in his article. That said, McGrath et al. (in press) attempted to justify these three dimensions as necessary, though perhaps not sufficient, components of a comprehensive model of character. Evidence was marshaled across educational, philosophical, and psychological literature supporting the ubiquity of these three factors in understanding successful functioning (e.g., Curren, 2008, 2013; National Research Council, 2012; Park, Tsukayama, Goodwin, Patrick, & Duckworth, 2016). My favorite piece of evidence that the model speaks to something fundamental in what makes us good people is L. Frank Baum's (1900/2006) *The Wonderful Wizard of Oz*. The story chronicles a search for a heart, a brain, and courage. In the end, of course, the protagonists find that the key to all three may be found within.

Since Nucci's model of moral character includes the concept of performance, the models do not seem that far apart. I see two key differences.

First, the omission of a component that focuses on intellectual curiosity limits his model's capacity for capturing moral functioning at its best. Without an element of regular reappraisal, moral beliefs will become complacent. It is reminiscent of Toni Morrison's (1987) *Beloved*, in which most of the White characters accept the inferior status of the Blacks without challenge. Even the siblings who appear to have rejected the status quo are oblivious to the implications of the racist figu-

rine they have on display in their house. As Erskine (1927) said, we have a moral obligation to be intelligent. In fact, I would consider inquisitiveness a necessary precursor to the formation of the capacity for discourse Nucci references as part of his model.

Second, the school of thought that equates character with morality tends to perceive concepts such as self-control and inquisitiveness as components of character only to the extent they contribute to moral functioning. The Aristotelian view instead considers these to be elements of good character in their own right, so long as they are not used for immoral ends. I believe evidence of self-control and inquisitiveness are likely to be taken as evidence of good character even in morally neutral situations. Productivity and curiosity deserve to be considered goods in themselves, contributors to the well-being of the individual, the quality of the individual's relationships, and the community in which the individual resides. It is not in service to morality that these attributes develop, though once developed they will serve morality as they do all other elements of the self-system. Character is something larger than morality, even if morality rests at its heart.

I will finish this section with some additional thoughts I have drawn from thinking about the model I have outlined here as it applies to character education in particular.

1. There is a tradition beginning with Aristotle of conceptualizing the virtues as reciprocal (Irwin, 1988), that is, they must all be present for true character to exist. Character education programs that focus on only some components of character are, I believe, inadequate to ensure a good person, and I think Dr. Nucci agrees with me here.

2. A comprehensive approach to teaching and encouraging development of the three key virtues of character would recognize three benefits that are likely to be important to the individual at different points in development. Virtuous behaviors benefit us personally, in that they help us flourish

in a social context. As Rosalind Hurst-house (1999) said, being virtuous is the only reliable bet we have for a happy life. Second, virtuous behaviors benefit our relationships. A surprising amount of Aristotle's *Nicomachean Ethics* is dedicated to friendship (Bartlett & Collins, 2007; see also Fowers, 2000). Finally, the products of our virtue contribute to the community as a whole. As a youth's world view widens, the reasons for virtue should broaden.

3. Nucci makes an important point in describing character as a relational developmental system. One of the most difficult tasks we face in becoming a moral person is figuring out the best moral choice in ambiguous and uncertain circumstances. This is a complex process, and we know very little still about how to transmit this knowledge to others. This statement provides the basis for my second point.

THE COMPLEXITIES OF CHARACTER

This second point has to do with whether Dr. Nucci has adequately captured the moral decision-making system. The organization of that system in terms of moral cognition, moral mental health, performance, and discourse is innovative. I would like to suggest, though, that this approach overlooks one of the most important issues that should be part of any program of moral/character education. Being moral is not inherently easy. It requires coming to a decision that balances a number of potentially competing considerations: care versus justice, sentiment versus contract, principle versus consequence, social responsibility versus self-preservation. I could go on at great length about each of these dilemmas, but given constraints of space, I hope the labels are sufficient to provide the reader with a sense of the dilemma each entails.

Compounding the problems is the practical matter of efficient versus deliberative decision-making; and our capacity to interpret prosocial behavior that comes at little cost, and is driven by contextual factors, as evidence of a firm moral identity. It is fortunate we so rarely face true moral dilemmas, where different considerations of roughly equal weight lead us to very different conclusions about what to do. If we did, claims of either consistency or coherence in our moral deliberations might be far weaker.

Unfortunately, the only perspective Nucci reviews that touches on this complexity is Haidt's (2012) moral foundations theory, which I agree with him is a very problematic model, for more reasons than he has outlined. However, the shortcomings of this model does not invalidate the importance of understanding, and of teaching students in character education programs to understand, the competing considerations that can enter into the practical process of moral decision-making. My point is that to understand how moral decision-making occurs in context, it is important not just to know what is right, it is also essential to know the methods by which we decide what is right in that context. For purposes of advancing the field of character education, this system of interlocking elements is the one that really matters.

CONCLUSIONS

To summarize, I think Dr. Nucci's article is thought-provoking and scholarly, and raises an intriguing new approach to thinking about the character system. It is this concept, of character as a system that operates within evolving contexts, that I consider his article's most important contribution. However, I think the system he describes could be improved in two ways.

First is its limitation to the moral. Should you consider it worthwhile to ask me, "what is virtuous character development," my answer might be broader than that Dr. Nucci would offer. I would say it involves people caring without the expectation of reciprocation, questioning their beliefs without a crisis, and demonstrating discipline even in the absence of structure. The enactment of character is a constant interchange between person and context, but I think these elements represent what a person of character would bring to that interchange.

Second is its minimization of issues of moral complexity and moral dilemma. Fortunately, stable societies are structured in such a way that acting in a relatively moral way is generally rewarded. The question is how we ensure that morality remains the dominant consideration when the immediate contingencies of reinforcement are otherwise. We must prepare people not only to be complacent moral agents when the moral choice is easy; we must think more about how to achieve moral decision-making when the moral choice is hard.

REFERENCES

Bartlett, R. C., & Collins, S. D. (2007). *Aristotle's nicomachean ethics*. Chicago, IL: University of Chicago Press.

Baum, L. F. (2006). *The wonderful wizard of Oz*. New York, NY: Signet. (Original work published 1900)

Berkowitz, M. W., Althof, W., & Bier, M. C. (2012). The practice of pro-social education. In P. M. Brown, M. W. Corrigan, & A. Higgins-D'Alessandro (Eds.), *The handbook of pro-social education* (pp. 71–90). Lanham, MD: Rowman & Littlefield.

Curren, R. (2008). Cardinal virtues of academic administration. *Theory and Research in Education, 6*, 337–363.

Curren, R. (2013). Aristotelian necessities. *The Good Society, 22*, 247–263.

Erskine, J. (1927). *American character and other essays*. Chautauqua, NY: Chautauqua Press.

Fowers, B. (2000). *Beyond the myth of marital happiness: How embracing the virtues of loyalty, generosity, justice, and courage can strengthen your relationship*. San Francisco, CA: Jossey-Bass.

Haidt, J. (2012). *The righteous mind: Why good people are divided by politics and religion*. New York, NY: Vintage.

Hursthouse, R. (1999). *On virtue ethics*. Oxford, England: Oxford University Press.

Irwin, T. H. (1988). Disunity in the Aristotelian virtues. In J. Annas (Ed.), *Oxford studies in ancient philosophy: Supplementary volume* (pp. 61–78). Oxford, England: Clarendon Press.

Kohlberg, L., & Hersh, R. H. (1977). Moral development: A review of the theory. *Theory Into Practice, 16*, 53–59.

Lerner, R. M., & Schmid Callina, K. (2014). The study of character development: Towards tests of a relational developmental systems model. *Human Development, 57*, 1–25.

Lickona, T., & Davidson, M. (2005). *Smart & good high schools: Integrating excellence and ethics for success in school, work, and beyond*. Cortland, NY: Center for the 4th and 5th Rs/Character Education Partnership. Retrieved from https://www2.cortland.edu/centers/character/high-schools/SnGReport.pdf

McAdams, D. P., & Manczak, E. (2015). Personality and the life story. In M. Mikulciner & P. R. Shaver (Eds.), *APA handbook of personality and social psychology: Vol. 4. Personality processes and individuals differences* (pp. 425–446). Washington, DC: American Psychological Association.

McAdams, D. P., & McLean, K. C. (2013). Narrative identity. *Current Directions in Psychological Science, 22*, 233–238.

McAdams, D. P., & Pals, J. L. (2006). A new Big Five: Fundamental principles for an integrative science of personality. *American Psychologist, 61*, 204–217.

McGrath, R. E. (2015). Integrating psychological and cultural perspectives on virtue: The hierarchical structure of character strengths. *Journal of Positive Psychology, 10*, 407–424.

McGrath, R. E. (2017). *What is character education? Development of a prototype*. Manuscript submitted for review.

McGrath, R. E., Greenberg, M. J., & Hall-Simmonds, A. (in press). Scarecrow, Tin Woodsman, and Cowardly Lion: The three-factor model of virtue. *Journal of Positive Psychology*.

Morrison, T. (1987). *Beloved*. New York, NY: Alfred A. Knopf.

National Research Council. (2012). *Education for life and work: Developing transferable knowl-*

edge and skills in the 21st century. Washington, DC: National Academies Press.

Park, D., Tsukayama, E., Goodwin, G. P., Patrick, S., & Duckworth, A. L. (2017). A tripartite taxonomy of character: Evidence for intrapersonal, interpersonal, and intellectual competencies in children. *Contemporary Educational Psychology, 48,* 16–27.

Peterson, C., & Seligman, M. E. P. (2004). *Character strengths and virtues: A classification and handbook.* Washington DC: American Psychological Association.

TOWARD A SCIENCE OF CHARACTER EDUCATION
Frameworks for Identifying and Implementing Effective Practices

Marvin W. Berkowitz and Melinda C. Bier
Center for Character and Citizenship, University of Missouri-St. Louis

Brian McCauley
Wasatch Academy (Utah)

A growing body of research on character education offers the opportunity to derive lessons on effective practice. While there is little focused research on the effectiveness of specific practices, reviews of effective programs have been mined for well over a decade to reach conclusions about "what works in character education." More recent reviews and meta-analyses offer the opportunity for a review of reviews. This article examines 8 reviews and identifies 42 evidence-based practices. However, such a list can be unwieldy by itself. Hence, a conceptual framework of 6 foundational character educational principles (PRIMED) is presented and used as an organizational structure for the 42 practices. In addition, a comparison is made of practices that have been shown to support academic achievement and those shown to foster character development, showing substantial overlap in effective academic and character practices.

Wanting to effectively promote the development of character is not equivalent to knowing how to do so. To build a science of character education, we must therefore ask, "What particular practices are supported by research as being effective?" In this article, drawing on a database of research literature collected from the variety of fields that inform character development in schools, we review what is scientifically known about the fostering of character development, especially as it applies to school settings. From previous research

• **Correspondence concerning this article should be addressed to:** Marvin W. Berkowitz, berkowitz@umsl.edu

Journal of Character Education, Volume 13(1), 2017, pp. 33–51
ISSN 1543-1223

reviews, we have concluded that there is very substantial overlap between family processes of character development and school-based processes of character development (Berkowitz, 2012; Berkowitz & Grych, 1998, 2000; Wentzel, 2002). In this review, we draw on both literatures, but much more heavily on the school-based literature. Our goal is to provide an updated, comprehensive picture of what works in school-based character education. We hope that our conclusions about effective practices and "frameworks" for effective implementation will be useful to multiple audiences, including researchers, institutions and organizations that prepare teachers and school leaders, educational policymakers, funders, and school practitioners.

DEFINING CHARACTER AND CHARACTER EDUCATION

Because others in this collection of articles are focusing on defining the field, we will only briefly discuss what we mean by "character" and "character education." Elsewhere, we have defined character education as "the intentional attempt in schools to foster the development of students' psychological characteristics that motivate and enable them to act in ethical, democratic, and socially effective and productive ways" (Berkowitz, Althof, & Bier, 2012, p. 72). It is important to note that we have long focused on the interpersonal, especially the *moral,* aspect of character; that is, one's motivation and capacity to do what is ethically right and socially responsible. However, character has been divided into at least four subcategories: moral, performance, intellectual, civic (Shields, 2011). It is beyond the scope of this paper to detail these complex and at times overlapping categories. We merely will state that here we will try to include as much of each of those "parts" of character as possible, and not limit ourselves to moral character. Hence, for this review, character is the set of psychological characteristics that motivate and enable one to function as a moral agent, to perform

optimally, to effectively pursue knowledge and intellectual flourishing, and to be an effective member of society.

WHAT DO WE MEAN BY "EFFECTIVE" CHARACTER EDUCATION?

We began the journey over 15 years ago to try to understand what is effective in promoting character in schools. When we began looking at what we called "What Works in Character Education?" (WWCE; Berkowitz & Bier, 2005), we had to grapple with what we would count as evidence of effectiveness. We ultimately settled on a fairly mainstream set of criteria. We felt that going with what was, at least at that time, the "gold standard" of randomized controlled trials (RCTs) would be setting the research design bar too high and that too few studies would meet those rigorous design criteria. That, in fact, turned out to be the case in the WWCE review. This was the strategy adopted by the U.S. Department of Education's (USDOE) What Works Clearinghouse (WWC; http://ies.ed.gov/ncee/wwc/default .aspx) later on, and they too found relatively few qualifying studies. In fact WWC stopped reviewing character education programs after 2007 and removed its summary review of this topic from the WWC website. RCTs were also the criterion for the Social and Character Development project, which generated very weak results for character education.

One argument against RCTs is that effective character education requires a whole school climate and philosophy that is authentically championed by the principal and embraced by the staff. That is something that is not amenable to be "randomly assigned." Hence we included various less rigorous research designs, such as many quasi-experimental designs. WWC, in 2015, offered a webinar on how to use such designs to meet their criteria, apparently recognizing that accepting only RCTs was inappropriate. It is beyond the scope of this paper to explicate our inclusion criteria; for more information see Berkowitz and Bier (2007). Jennifer Urban and her colleagues have done school-based evaluation a great service in their recent work articulating the theoretical and practical problems associated with the current, almost exclusive enthusiasm for RCTs and the policy-driven mandates for evidence-based programming. They provide a theory-based and intellectually appealing framework, Evolutionary Evaluation, for designing, aligning and valuing program evaluation appropriately (Urban, Hargraves, & Trochim, 2014).

Ultimately, in this paper, "effective" means a practice that is supported by scientific evidence including statistical tests of the significance of the impact. We also include only studies that measure some aspect of character (widely defined) as an outcome. Many reviews focus on character implementation but measure only academic outcomes (e.g., Darling-Hammond, 2002; Yeager & Walton, 2011), and hence are not included in this review of character education. Instead, those studies will be mentioned in a later section of this paper that identifies parallels between what is found to be effective in promoting character development and what is found to be effective in promoting academic achievement. What we mainly want to know is what promotes character development, rather than "What does character education, broadly defined, impact?" That is an important question, but not our focus in this paper.

WHAT WE INCLUDE
IN OUR SEARCH
FOR "EFFECTIVE PRACTICES"

There are many choices of how to select and organize research of relevance to such a review. Ultimately, it is very difficult to find research studies that isolate specific classroom or schoolwide strategies and measure their impact on character outcomes. Hence we have had to employ a set of tangential approaches. First, we look for those few strategies that have

been extensively studied in isolation. In WWCE (Berkowitz & Bier, 2005) we chose two: moral dilemma discussion and cooperative learning. Research on other strategies can now be added; that is, mindfulness and service learning. However, it is well beyond the scope of this review to summarize the growing research on specific strategies or practices (terms that we use interchangeably in this paper), but it would be very helpful in the future for such a compilation to be amassed and disseminated, just as it would be to amass the evidence for what effects specific outcomes.

The second approach we have taken is to look at the prevalence of specific strategies across effective programs. In WWCE, we defined programs loosely as multifaceted approaches to character education with defined practices, and generally well-defined, documented, named and disseminated, although this is not a formal or rigid set of criteria, but rather a guideline. We found that such programs averaged almost eight separate strategies per program. This led us to create a list of effective strategies in WWCE. This is a coarse approximation of effectiveness, because there is no way to disentangle the confounded strategies within a given program, and hence across programs. In this paper, we have chosen to mostly do a review of reviews, in the spirit of John Hattie's impressive review of hundreds of meta-analyses of research on education effectiveness (Hattie, 2009), but far less systematically and ambitiously than what he was able to accomplish.

In searching for reviews of literature relevant to identifying effective character education practices, we found that there are not that many. Some reviews looked only at academic outcomes (e.g., Yeager & Walton, 2011), some only reviewed programs and not specific strategies (e.g., Public Profit, 2014), et cetera. There simply is little systematic review of individual pedagogical strategies that are effective in fostering the development of character. Clearly, more research is needed. Nonetheless, we have continued to add to our conclusions from WWCE (Berkowitz & Bier, 2005) in subsequent reviews (Berkowitz, 2011a; Berkowitz & Bier, 2014), and are expanding it further here by including newly identified reviews and reviews of relevant research in related fields, most specifically socioemotional learning and positive psychology.

We have settled on eight sources for this compilation and analysis. Not included are reviews that look only at programs and not specific practices; such as, Public Profit's (2014) review of 16 programs that promote noncognitive skills or Heckman and Kautz's (2014) review of character programs that are efficacious for life outcomes. Also not included are reviews of character education programs which only report their impact on academic achievement (e.g., Benninga, Berkowitz, Kuehn, & Smith, 2003; Yeager & Walton, 2011). The eight sources we included are as follows:

1. We have, for over 15 years, been collecting and filtering individual studies that meet our criteria. That in fact was the basis of the first report on WWCE (Berkowitz & Bier, 2005, 2007). More recently we completed a transition from a simple word-processing data base to a web-based database (Character Education Research Clearinghouse, https://characterandcitizenship.org/home-cerch). We began WWCE by hoping to broadly look for evidence of effective practices, but found, with a couple of notable exceptions, that most of the qualifying empirical research examined the impact of entire multifaceted programs and not specific implementation strategies. When we ended our search in 2004, we found evidence for 33 effective programs. Subsequently (Berkowitz, 2011a), we have attempted to expand the findings from WWCE to include research on parenting impacts on character development as well as the findings of other groups such as the Collaborative for Academic, Social and Emotional Learning (CASEL; www.casel.org).

2. CASEL, in their Safe and Sound review (2005), which was intentionally a review of programs, found 80 programs and identified "22 that are especially strong and effective" (p. i). They have also published a meta-analysis of 213 interventions (Durlak et al., 2011). More recently, they have prepared a set of "guides" with more comprehensive, focused, and up-to-date reviews (e.g., CASEL, 2015).

3. Character.org's flagship model is the *Eleven Principles of Effective Character Education* (Beland, 2003), which is a model based on extensive reviews of the research and practice literatures.

4. Lovat, Toomey, Dally, and Clement (2009), while not reviewing research findings, extensively studied effective schools in Australia and generated a list of best practices.

5. Leming (1997) reviewed effective programs and distilled effective practices from them, much as WWCE did.

6. Lickona has been collecting examples and research for over a quarter of a century which has resulted in many publications (Lickona, 1991, 2004). His team's work on effective high schools is used here (Davidson, Lickona & Khmelkov, 2008; Lickona & Davidson, 2005).

7. The U.S. Department of Education (2013) published a review of research on educating for grit, tenacity, and perseverance which identified specific practices.

8. The National School Climate Center (www.schoolclimate.org) has many frameworks for fostering character and socioemotional development through the creation of positive school climates. We use their basic model of four key strategies here.

EFFECTIVE CHARACTER EDUCATION PRACTICES

When considering what influences school implementation of character education, it is important to keep in mind that schools do not exist in vacuums, just as classrooms are not islands of practice. Most schools and classrooms conform to established norms, even if those norms prescribe ineffective practices. There are exceptions, of course; some teachers can find ways to deviate from the norms and resist contextual pressures to use ineffective practices (e.g., Berger, 2003; Urban, 2008), and schools can do likewise (e.g., Berkowitz, Pelster, & Johnston, 2012; Johnston, 2012). More commonly, however, educational practice is greatly influenced by forces outside the school (e.g., the school district), and even outside the district (e.g., state or national educational policy, economics, etc.). We will not look beyond the school in this review, as it is beyond our expertise and beyond our scope. Furthermore, when looking at the school, one can differentiate between "whole school" strategies that are implemented at the school level and those that are merely ubiquitous but implemented at the classroom level (e.g., when a program or strategy is delivered in every classroom). In other words, this can be murky and complex. Given the relatively nascent state of the literature, such fine-grained distinctions may not be helpful or even viable, so we will proceed with a broad brush and ask forgiveness for any blurring of lines.

In the search for effective practices, one can start with specific practices, and see what outcomes they appear to cause—as in the case of the reviews of cooperative learning (e.g., Johnson & Johnson, 1987) or service learning (e.g., Billig, 2002). A second approach is to look at effective programs and ask what they impact and what individual strategies they include—as was done in WWCE (Berkowitz & Bier, 2005). A third approach is to start with specific outcomes and examine what research tells us about the factors causing them—as was done in the USDOE's report on promoting grit, tenacity, and perseverance (USDOE, 2013).

A fourth approach is to try to identify broad underlying principles of effective character education and use those both as a conceptual framework and a scheme for clustering empirical findings on effective practices. We find this fourth approach to be perhaps the most useful way of making sense of the research on character education effectiveness and will use this approach in the remainder of this article. We think that this approach has the greatest potential for helping the field think broadly and deeply about what effective character education is, in a way that stimulates further discussion and research on this critical question.

FRAMEWORKS FOR IDENTIFYING AND IMPLEMENTING EFFECTIVE PRACTICES

By 'framework" we mean a conceptual system, a set of ideas, that has links to a research base but is more than just a list of "effective practices." It is a higher order way of thinking about discrete effective practices that sets forth general principles—"big ideas"—that in turn enable us to cluster effective practices, provide broad guidance for implementation, and identify where more research is needed in order to clarify our understanding of what makes for optimally effective character education.

Character.org, the predominant character education organization, has used as its flagship guidelines *The Eleven Principles of Effective Character Education* (11P) since at least 1996 (www.character.org). CASEL has offered its *SAFE* criteria for effective practice, encompassing four key principles: Sequenced activities within a coordinate curriculum; Active pedagogy aimed as mastery of SEL skills; Focused component of the school that targets SEL skills; Explicit targeting of specific SEL skills. That National School Climate Center (www.schoolclimate.org) offers many such frameworks for understanding school climate.

A different framework, one focused on meeting basic psychological needs, comes from self-determination theory (Deci & Ryan, 2002). Self-determination theory posits three fundamental human psychological needs—for autonomy, belonging and competence—and maintains that effective education can happen only when schools target and effectively fulfill these needs. From an educational perspective, this should lead to a consideration of what educational strategies are necessary to promote the fulfillment of these needs. For example, Reeve and Halusic (2009) have articulated the characteristics of an "autonomy-supportive classroom": "take the students' perspective, display patience to allow time for learning, nurture inner motivation resources, provide explanatory rationales, rely on noncontrolling language, and acknowledge and accept expressions of negative affect" (p. 145).

Still another framework, one we have derived from our ongoing review of the research is called PRIME (Berkowitz, 2009; Berkowitz & Bier, 2014; Berkowitz & Bustamante, 2013), an acronym for five principles of effective character education: Prioritizing character education as central to the school's (or classroom's) mission and purpose; promoting positive Relationships among all school stakeholders; fostering the internalization of positive values and virtues through Intrinsic motivational strategies; Modeling character by adults; emphasizing a pedagogy of Empowerment which gives authentic voice to all stakeholders (see Table 1).

In doing this review, we identified all the effective practices in all the sources we examined and then made a master list of them. We found we could categorize almost all of these evidence-based strategies into one of the five concepts of PRIME. We added a sixth category (developmental pedagogy) to incorporate the rest of the strategies that did not easily fit

PRIME; in effect changing PRIME to PRIMED.

Prioritization. Character education needs to be an authentic priority in the school. This includes being central to seminal statements such as mission and vision statements. It also includes leadership that has both the capacity and competency to lead a school to effective implementation as well as the inclination to do so. It also requires an investment in the professional development of all key stakeholders (Berkowitz & Bier, 2005; Darling-Hammond, 2002). A shared language and set of values that are explicit and, ideally, consensual should undergird and frame the initiative. Schools and classrooms need to intentionally foster the development of climates that feel safe to students, that care for and include all, and that strive for justice in discipline and the distribution of resources.

The prioritization strategies identified in this research review are grouped into five subcategories: (1) rhetorical emphasis; (2) allocation of resources; (3) school and classroom climate; (4) schoolwide structures; (5) leadership (see Table 2).

Relationships. The strategic and intentional nurturing of relationships is foundational for effective practice. School structures and schedules that are dedicated to relationship building must be intentionally implemented to support the formation of such relationships. All stakeholders and their interrelationships should be included in this relational focus. Schools should connect to and leverage nonschool community members and organiza-

TABLE 1
Six Principles of the PRIMED Model

Prioritization: Prioritization of character and social emotional development in school

Relationships: Strategic and intentional promotion of healthy relationships among all school stakeholders

Intrinsic Motivation: Promotion of the internalization of core values/virtues through intrinsic motivational strategies

Modeling: All adults and older students model core values/virtues and socioemotional competencies

Empowerment: Schools empower all stakeholders as co-owners and coauthors of the character education initiative and the school in general

Developmental Pedagogy: Schools intentionally foster the development of student character and socioemotional competence and utilize methods that are developmental in purpose

TABLE 2
PRIMED, Subcategories, and Implementation Strategies

PRIMED Principle	Subcategory	Implementation Strategy
Prioritization	Rhetoric	• Core values/shared goals/common language
	Resources	• Leadership allocation of resources to character education
		• Intentionally creating a learning community
		• Investing in professional development for char education
	Climate	• Safe environment
		• Assess school culture/climate
		• Trust in teachers
		• Schoolwide character education culture/focus
		• Caring classroom/school climate
	Structures	• Comprehensive approach to character education
		• School displays/awards
		• Clear rules
		• Assessment and feedback for character/SEL
		• Interschool collaboration
	Leadership	• Principal competently leads the initiative
Relationships	Within school	• Peer interactive pedagogical methods
		• Intentional promotion of relationships
		• Peer conflict resolution program
		• Nurturing adults
		• Teaching relationship skills
	Beyond the school	• Relationships with families and/or community
Intrinsic motivation	Behavior management	• Developmental discipline
		• Induction/empathy
		• Praise effort, not ability
		• Use of reflection (especially moral)
	Self-growth	• Challenging/meaningful/relevant curriculum
		• Opportunities for revising one's work/efforts
		• Goal setting/Imagining possible selves
	Service	• Opportunities for moral action
		• Community service/Service learning
Modeling		• Role modeling/mentoring
		• Studying others as role models/exemplars
Empowerment		• Shared leadership
		• Democratic classrooms
		• Culture of empowerment/collaboration
		• Fair and respectful of students
Developmental pedagogy	Teaching character	• Teaching about character
		• Teaching socioemotional (SEL) competencies
		• Curricular integration
	Expectations for growth	• High expectations/focus on excellence
		• Mental contrasting with implementation intention
	Practice	• Role playing/practice

tions. This includes parent involvement, but also includes local government, local business, law enforcement, community organizations, et cetera (Darling-Hammond, 2002). The relationship-supportive strategies identified in this review are clustered into two subcategories: (1) within school; (2) beyond school.

Intrinsic Motivation (Internalization). Strategies should be selected for their power to lead to the authentic internalization of the specific values and virtues that the initiative is designed to foster, as well as authentic personal commitment to the socioemotional competencies being targeted. Ultimately, strategies that support intrinsic motivation, the development of a prosocial identity, and virtue should be identified and selected for implementation. Internalization strategies identified in this review are clustered into three subcategories: (1) behavior management strategies; (2) strategies for self-growth; (3); opportunities to serve others.

Role Models. All adults who exist in the school environment need to model what they want students to be and do. Students need to also be exposed to other role models, especially including exemplars and covering all aspects of good character—performance, civic, intellectual, civic and moral character. Such models can be older students, community members, historical figures, and fictional characters in literature. There were no subcategories of modeling.

Pedagogy of Empowerment. Schools need to flatten their governance structures and honor the voices of all stakeholders by sharing power and institutionalizing structures and practices that are more democratic and less authoritarian and hierarchical. In essence, this is a matter of respect for personhood and meeting the fundamental autonomy needs of all school members, while also serving citizenship development in a democratic society (Althof & Berkowitz, 2006). There were no subcategories of empowerment.

Developmental Pedagogy. Students' needs should be understood and met, particularly through the strategies implemented.

These include challenge, autonomy, belonging, competence, and relevance. The developmental strategies identified in this review are grouped into three subcategories: (1) direct teaching of character; (2) Expectations for student development; (3) Opportunities to practice and master new competencies.

IMPLEMENTATION STRATEGIES

As noted above, there is little empirical guidance for specific isolated effective pedagogical strategies. The most specific lists come from nonsystematic (i.e., no formal search and review protocols) or quasi-empirical reviews (i.e., combining research-supported practices with non-research-based practices) (e.g., Beland, 2003; Berkowitz, 2011a; Darling-Hammond, 2002; Lickona & Davidson, 2005) or from extrapolations from empirical data (e.g., reaching conclusions about effectiveness by being present in broader effective programs; Berkowitz & Bier, 2005). These types of reviews therefore will serve as the basis for our conclusions. The reviews have been synthesized and a list of all supported implementation strategies have both generated the above listed six principles and supported the organization of the specific strategies within the six principles and their subcategories, which is how they will be presented here (see Table 2). The subcategories do not represent a theory of the nature of the six principles; rather they are the best conceptual clustering of specific implementation strategies determined to align with a specific principle.

Prioritization

Prioritization is about focusing authentically on nurturing the development of character both in students and in the school (or classroom) as an organization. It is an organizational analogy to the idea of individual noble purpose (Damon, 2008). There are five interrelated ways to manifest the priority of character education in a school, which we depict as five subcategories of the principle of prioritization in Table 2.

1. **Rhetoric.** Perhaps the easiest way to prioritize character education and development is through the language of the school. Having a shared or common language is often recognized and implemented in schools to varying degrees. This is most typically a set of core values, virtues, socioemotional competencies, or character strengths, as suggested in the first principle of the Character.org *Eleven Principles of Effective Character Education* (www.character.org). Beyond the 11 principles, it was also emphasized in four other reviews included in this report. Often however, such words are, in actual practice, merely "words on a wall" and have little impact on the actual functioning of the school. Effective practice includes wide understanding of the words, operational definitions, behavioral anchoring, and even rubrics (Johnston, 2012). Then the words are used widely and incorporated throughout school functioning; e.g., discipline, academic curricula.

2. **Allocation of Resources.** It is far easier to proclaim prioritization of character than it is to actually allocate resources accordingly. We identified three strategies for prioritization through the allocation of resources. (1) CASEL reported that the allocation of resources by school leadership was essential to the effective promotion of socioemotional competencies in students (www.casel.org). (2) One specific place to allocate resources is to the professional development of staff in ways that support the competency to engage in effective character education. Berkowitz and Bier (2005) reported that all 33 effective character education programs had at least optional professional development, and this was also found to be supportive of the development of GRIT (USDOE, 2013). (3) One specific way to support

staff professional development and effective implementation is to intentionally foster a learning community, or, as Lickona and Davidson (2005) call it, a professional ethical learning community.

3. **School Climate.** The National School Climate Center (www.schoolclimate.org) has articulated and emphasized the importance of a sociological perspective on character education; that is, seeing character development as a product of the social organization of the classroom and/or school. It has also reviewed the research on the impact of school climate on both academics and socioemotional and character development (Thapa, Cohen, Higgins-D'Alessandro, & Guffey, 2012). While various aspects of school climate are discussed, this review revealed five specific strategies of relevance. (1) Six of the eight reviews highlighted the need for a clear schoolwide culture or focus on character education. (2) Trust in teachers supports effective character education. (3) An environment that is psychologically and physically safe, and is perceived as such by school members, was identified by CASEL (2015). (4) The National School Climate Center, Character.org, and Lickona all have identified the promotion of caring schools and classrooms as supportive of character development and socioemotional competencies. (5) Lastly, assessing school climate is part of Character.org's final principle of effective character education and is a centerpiece for the National School Climate Center's work.

4. **Structural Prioritization.** Schools can be restructured in ways that increase the presence and prioritization of character education. Oftentimes best intentions are not realized because no specific structures are created to support and/or sustain such intentions. Research supports five different ways of structuring for character education. (1) Character.org emphasizes making character education comprehen-

sive, so that it impacts all aspects of development (Principle 2) and is integrated in all aspects of the school (Principle 3). (2) Having clear rules that are widely known was reported by CASEL. (3) Lovat et al. (2009) noted that schools collaborating for character education was an effective strategy. (4) Lovat et al. also identified making character and character education visible and salient through displays and awards. (5) Assessing character and giving students feedback on their behavior was identified by the USDOE (2013).

5. **Leadership.** Leadership is the one area of practice that was not identified in any of the reviews, but is still included here. In the literature on academic success, school leadership is found to be critical (e.g., Leithwood, Harris & Hopkins, 2008; Marzano, Waters, & McNulty, 2001). The same sentiments tend to be echoed in the role of schools in character development (Berkowitz, 2011b); however little research has been done to examine the role of school leadership in promoting character development. There are case studies (e.g., Berkowitz et al., 2012; Johnston, 2012), but very little scientific research (an exception is Marshall, Caldwell, & Foster, 2011) to support this. Recently a team at the Center for Character and Citizenship has examined the characteristics of effective character education principals and linked those to the use of effective practices and to school climate (Frugo, Johnston, McCauley, & Navarro, 2016). The Leadership Academy in Character Education in St. Louis, led by the first author, has spawned more National Schools of Character than any single entire state in the US. For these reasons, we include leadership as a prioritization strategy; however, more research is needed on this topic. Berkowitz (2011b) has suggested that leaders need to understand character, character development and character education, be instructional leaders for it, model good character, and

empower all stakeholders in the school to share in the responsibility of effectively fostering character and socioemotional development in students. Finally, it is important to note that, while this discussion focuses on formal leadership (i.e., individuals in positions defined as leadership roles) which is the ideal locus for institutional change, leadership in character education can potentially come from other stakeholders including students, teachers, support staff, and parents.

Relationships

Relationships are foundational to good schools and the promotion of character and socioemotional development. It is worth noting that relationships will not happen widely, but rather selectively, if they are not a strategic goal of the school, and hence strategically built into school processes, policies, and structures. While we are mainly interested in building relationships within the school, the review did reveal one common strategy that goes beyond the boundaries of the school, and that is included in this report, hence generating two subcategories of this principle: Within School; and Beyond School.

1. **Within School Relationship Strategies**. Because relationships are so foundational, this review revealed five different approaches to promoting positive relationships within the school. (1) Both CASEL and the National School Climate Center simply recommend the promotion of healthy relationships. (2) There should be an emphasis on pedagogical strategies that require peer interaction; e.g., cooperative learning, class meetings, peer tutoring, moral dilemma discussion, et cetera. WWCE, CASEL, Leming, and Lickona all highlight this strategy. It is worth noting that both of the specifically studied strategies identified in WWCE (cooperative learning and moral dilemma discussions) are peer interactive strategies.

Moral dilemma discussions are a special case as they are designed for a single specific outcome; the development of moral reasoning capacities (moral critical thinking), which, while studied more extensively than almost any other specific strategy, nonetheless tends to be underemphasized in much of the character education literature. Moral dilemma discussions could also be listed under the "D" of PRIMED (Developmental Pedagogy) as they are designed to nurture the long-term development of moral critical thinking capacities. (3) The use of an effective peer conflict resolution program was identified by CASEL and Lickona as an effective practice. (4) WWCE identified teachers' nurturing relationships with and attitudes toward students as effective in promoting character and socioemotional development. (5) Both CASEL and Lovat et al. specifically pointed to nurturing the development of relationship skills. This strategy could have been placed in more than one category; such as, it is a socioemotional competency and hence could have been subsumed within the final principle. However, given the centrality of relationships and its mention in two reviews, it is included separately and under the principle of relationships.

2. **Beyond School**. One of the more commonly reported strategies is the promotion of school to family and school to community relationships. This was specifically identified in four of the reviews.

Intrinsic Motivation (Internalization of Character)

Ultimately, the goal of character education is for children and adolescents to become good people, to develop into and act effectively as agents for good in the world. Hence this is as much about *being* people of character as it is about *acting* good. Both are essential. This is where so many schools go awry—by relying on strategies that shape behavior, but are not equally effective in nurturing the inner character that is the source of virtuous behavior.

The goal of authentic character education should be the internalization of values and virtues that motivate and guide one's behavior, along with the socioemotional competencies to enact those internalized characteristics. Character.org echoes Lickona (2004) and others in defining character as having a cognitive (knowledge, reasoning) component, an affective/motivational component, and a behavioral component. It is the affective/motivational component that requires internalization that in turn leads to intrinsic motivation to act out of those values and virtues. The promotion of such intrinsic motivation requires a specific set of strategies (Streight, 2015). We have clustered the strategies for promoting intrinsic motivation into three subcategories: management of student behavior; promotion of personal growth; service to others.

1. **Management of Student Behavior.** One of the great challenges of schooling is to help students behave in ways that are safe, prosocial, and conducive to learning. The range of options is wide (e.g., Deci, Koestner, & Ryan, 1999). Doing so in order to promote intrinsic motivation, however, has been linked to a specific set of practices. Four strategies for managing behavior were found in this review. (1) Developmental discipline (Watson, 2003) was identified by WWCE and Lovat et al. (2009). How undesirable behavior is understood and responded to should align with the practices of developmental discipline. It should be done to promote rather than undermine relationships. It should be construed and approached as an opportunity to nurture the long-term positive development of the child, including to enhance and practice healthy SEL competencies. It should be done in ways that empower the child to take responsibility for his/her actions and to repair the damage those actions caused. It should rely on ensuring

that students understand why their behavior is inappropriate and how it has impacted others and particularly their emotions. (2) The use of induction to foster empathy was identified by WWCE and CASEL. (3) Praising effort and not ability was identified by the USDOE study of GRIT. (4) The promotion of reflection (especially about morality and character) was identified by four reviews.

2. **Promotion of Personal Growth.** Another way to foster the internalization of character strengths and increasing the intrinsic motivation to be a moral agent is to specifically target strategies that promote personal growth. It should be noted that this cluster overlaps with the "D" in PRIMED (Developmental Pedagogy) but the examples used here seem particularly related to fostering intrinsic motivation. (1) Having a challenging and meaningful academic curriculum aligns with the frequent finding in both the parenting (Berkowitz & Grych, 1998) and education (e.g., Wentzel, 2002) literatures that scaffolded high expectations are highly successful in promoting both character and learning. Character.org, Lovat et al. (2009), and the USDOE identified a challenging and meaningful/relevant curriculum as an effective strategy. (2) Providing opportunities to redo one's efforts, both academic and behavioral, was identified by the USDOE and Lickona. (3) Helping students identify and set goals for themselves was identified by the USDOE review. This can include reflecting on one's ideal self (future self, possible self) and crafting a plan to move toward it. This includes Darling-Hammond's (2002) identification of "personalization" as one of the principles of what works in academically successful small high schools, which, in turn, aligns with the widely found conclusion that high expectations for both academics and development are necessary for effective development (Ber-

kowitz & Grych, 2000; Darling-Hammond, 2002).

3. **Service to Others.** There should be many opportunities for all students to serve others. This can be done through formal roles in the school, such as student government. It can be done through peer relationships, such as peer tutoring or teaching advisory class lessons. Two strategies were identified. (1) Providing opportunities for moral action was one of the most frequently identified strategies, with five reviews identifying it. (2) Two reviews WWCE and Lickona and Davidson) specifically identified serving others through community service or service learning. Service learning is one of the few strategies that has also been well-researched in isolation (e.g., Billig, 2002).

Modeling

In the parenting literature, it is well established that parents need to not only use parenting strategies that foster specific character outcomes, but they need also to model those outcomes (Berkowitz & Grych, 1998). This is true as well for educators, but it is often a difficult pill to swallow (Berkowitz, 2012). Nonetheless, this review found many examples of evidence for the necessity for educators to "walk the character talk." All of them clustered into two strategies, and were hence not clustered into superordinate subcategories.

1. **Role Modeling/Mentoring.** Students should be provided with ample models of character. This most centrally includes the adults in the school (and oftentimes older students as well). Five reviews identified role modeling and mentoring as an effective practice in fostering the development of character and socioemotional competencies.

2. **Studying Role Models.** Students can also learn from role models beyond the school, such as figures in society and history, and figures in literature, but individ-

uals in the local community too. The Giraffe Project (www.giraffe.org) is an excellent example of a specific curriculum for using heroes to foster character development. Lickona and Davidson identified this as an "effective practice."

Pedagogy of Empowerment

Hierarchical and authoritarian school practices should be transformed to incorporate appropriate opportunities for student voice (Althof & Berkowitz, 2006; Berkowitz, 2012; Darling-Hammond, 2002). This also aligns with the autonomy-supportive classroom model of self-determination theory (Ryan & Deci, 2013). There were four specific strategies identified in this review that support the promotion of empowerment, but they did not generate superordinate subcategories. (1) General empowerment and collaboration was identified by WWCE, CASEL, and the USDOE. (2) More specifically, shared leadership was identified by Character.org and Lovat et al. (2009). (3) Creating democratic classrooms was a practice identified by Lickona. (4) Finally, the USDOE also identified being fair to and respectful of students.

Developmental Pedagogy

After sorting all the evidence-based strategies for promoting the development of character and socioemotional competencies into the five principles of PRIME, six strategies remained. These have been clustered under the rubric of Developmental Pedagogy, because all seem to focus on the direct promotion of positive development. Hence this review has generated a sixth principle for the PRIME model and turning it into PRIMED. In turn, the six strategies have been clustered into three subcategories: teaching character; expectations for growth; practice.

1. **Teaching Character.** There are three strategies aligned with teaching character and socioemotional development. (1) The direct and targeted teaching of character was identified by WWCE, Lovat et al., Lickona and Davidson, and the National School Climate Center. (2) In parallel, the direct teaching of socioemotional competencies was identified by WWCE, CASEL, Lickona and Davidson, and the National School Climate Center. (3) Providing opportunities for students to practice and master these competencies, often through role-playing, was specifically identified by the USDOE, CASEL, and Leming.

2. **Expectations for Growth/Development.** There were two strategies identified that target the promotion of general development or growth. (1) In alignment with much research on both parenting and education, four reviews (WWCE, CASEL, Lovat et al., Lickona) identified setting high expectations (for academics and/or character). (2) The USDOE reported that mental contrasting effectively promotes persistence. Mental Contrasting (Oettingen, 2000) in combination with Implementation Intention (Gollwitzer, 1999) is a strategy developed and tested under the name MCII (Oettingen & Gollwitzer, 2009) and commercialized under the name WOOP that asks students to compare the idea of a desired future state with obstacles that they envision might impede their progress toward that state and to construct if–then scenarios for how they might overcome each obstacle (Duckworth, Grant, Loew, Oettingen, & Gollwitzer, 2011).

Practice. The use of the specific developmental strategy of practicing desired competencies and strengths, including the particular use of role-playing, was identified by three reviews: CASEL, Leming, and USDOE.

DISTRIBUTION OF PRACTICES WITHIN PRIMED FRAMEWORK

It may be useful to also look at indicators of prevalence of inclusion of a practice in reviews of research as a proxy for degree of impact on character development. Without meta-analyses and other effect size analyses, it is impossible to directly measure relative impact of the strategies, but looking at frequency of identification may be an index of impact. Of course, this is a coarse metric, as frequency could also be a product of popularity not born of effectiveness, so we do this analysis with that cautionary thought in mind. At the macro level (PRIMED principles), Prioritization has both the most total mentions (26) and the most specific strategies (15) of the six principles. Intrinsic Motivation/Internalization is second in both mentions (22) and strategies (9). Third is Developmental Pedagogy with 18 mentions and 6 strategies. Relationships had 14 mentions and was tied with Developmental Pedagogy with 6 strategies. Empowerment had 7 mentions and 4 strategies, and Modeling has 6 mentions and 2 strategies.

Another way to look at prevalence of inclusion in reviews is to look at the microlevel of specific strategies. Seventeen of the 42 strategies were identified by only one of the eight reviews (as noted, leadership was included in this report even though it was not specifically mentioned by any of the eight reviews). Ten more were identified by two of the reviews. Of the 14 practices that were mentioned by more than two of the eight reviews, only having a schoolwide culture of character or schoolwide focus on character was mentioned by as many as six reviews. There were five mentions each for only three of the practices: (1) have a set of core values and/or shared language, (2) providing opportunities for moral action, and (3) adults and/or older students acting as role models and/or mentors. Five more practices were identified by four of the eight reviews: (1) family and/or community involvement; (2) teaching about character; (3) teaching socioemotional competencies (SEL); (4) having high expectations. Five more practices were each mentioned by three of the reviews: (1) professional development; (2) use of peer interactive strategies; (3) having a challenging, meaningful, relevant curriculum; (4) empow-ering and collaborating with others; (5) use of role-play and practice.

PARALLELS TO FINDINGS ON PRACTICES THAT PROMOTE ACADEMIC SUCCESS

As noted at the outset, the selection of reviews for this paper excluded those for which the sole dependent variable was academic achievement or other measures of academic success. Nonetheless, it is interesting to look at the contrast of what such reviews (which are far more plentiful than those focusing on character and/or socioemotional outcomes) report as effective evidence-based practices. It is beyond the scope of this paper to review all such summary analyses. Rather, for the sake of this intellectual exercise, four reviews were selected. Hattie's *Visible Learning* project (Hattie, 2009; Hattie & Yates, 2014) is the most comprehensive review of reviews and well beyond summarizing briefly; however, selected findings from that project will be included here. Specifically, those that correspond to the findings in this review will be incorporated. Marzano (2003) has, like Hattie, reviewed massive amounts of research to distill best practices in school success. Benninga et al. (2003) looked at aspects of schools that applied for recognition of academic excellence and identified character education practices that correlated with academic success. Darling-Hammond (2002) looked for the characteristics of small high schools that led to academic success.

Of the 42 practices identified as supportive of character and socioemotional development, 30 were specifically identified in one or more of the four academic outcome reviews included in this comparison (11 of those 30 were cited in more than one of the four academic outcome reviews). Perhaps more importantly, each of the six key principles of PRIMED was cited at least once, as were every one of the subcategories of all of the six principles. In other words, the entire overall model of PRIMED including its subcategories were represented in this review of effective practices for academic success, even though only four sources were incorporated here.

The 12 character education strategies that were not represented in the academic outcome literature reviewed here include two broad types of strategies: (1) those that could logically apply to academic outcome research; and (2) those that are particular to character outcome research and would not be expected to be identified in academic success reviews or studies. The six strategies that could apply to academic outcome research that were not cited in the academic outcome reviews are: (1) assessing school culture; (2) creating a caring climate in classrooms and schools; (3) schools working together; (4) developmental discipline; (5) teaching goal setting; (6) mental contrasting. Of these six, only developmental discipline was identified by more than one of the eight character outcome reviews; that is, these were low frequency implementation strategies in the set of character education reviews. Furthermore, while they may apply to academic success, strategies such as creating a caring climate or developmental discipline are not typically invoked in academic school improvement theories or interventions.

A clear example of how such strategies can be found to relate to academic outcomes if they are studied for academic impact is the work of Bryk and Schneider (2002) finding that the relational trust among teachers strongly predicts student academic achievement. Such research, along with the rapidly growing literature demonstrating the impact of character education broadly (Benninga et al., 2003), sociemotional learning in particular (Durlak et al., 2011), and performance character (also mislabeled as "soft skills" and "noncognitive skills"; e.g., Duckworth, 2016; Tough, 2012), all suggest the need for more research on the relation of character education to academic outcomes.

The six strategies that are particular to character education that were unsurprisingly not cited in the four academic outcome reviews because they are by definition linked to char-

acter development are: (1) leadership allocation of resources to character education; (2) a comprehensive approach to character education; (3) use of induction and focus on empathy in behavior management; (4) studying others as moral role models; (5) integrating character education into the academic curriculum; (6) use of school displays about character and character awards. Of these, only curricular integration was identified by more than one of the eight character outcome reviews. Again, these are relatively low frequency strategies in the literature on evidence-based character education.

CONCLUSIONS

Ultimately, the success of attempts to promote the development of character and socioemotional competencies in students will rest on the ability to identify and then effectively implement evidence-based practices. This paper is the next step in an ongoing project to identify and disseminate such practices, which began with the *What Works in Character Education* project (Berkowitz & Bier, 2005), and has continued with the establishment of the Character Education Resource Clearinghouse. We have attempted to update our sources and in this project to utilize a set of eight review projects to identify research-based practices. We have organized them around six broad principles of effective practice (PRIMED): (1) authentically prioritizing character education in schools; (2) strategically and intentionally promoting positive relationships among all school stakeholders; (3) nurturing the internalization of character strengths/values/virtues resulting in intrinsic motivation; (4) modeling character and socioemotional competencies; (5) empowering all stakeholders to be co-owners and coauthors of the initiative; (6) employing a developmental pedagogy. This has led to a list of 42 character education implementation strategies which have research evidence to support their effectiveness specifically in promoting character and socioemotional development.

Interestingly, but not surprisingly, a brief review of major synopses of the research on effective (for academic outcomes) schools shows appreciable overlap in the strategies supported for both academic outcomes and character and socioemotional outcomes. Furthermore, the 14 most identified implementation strategies in the character outcome reviews were all cited in at least one of the academic outcome reviews. In other words, as we have long opined when introducing character education to educators, "good character education is good education."

What is needed is more systematic research on specific strategies and meta-analyses of the studies included in the various reviews. While there is substantial research on a very small set of individual strategies (e.g., service learning, moral dilemma discussion, cooperative learning), most of the strategies are only studied as part of multifaceted character education initiatives. This was a challenge 15 years ago when we began the WWCE project and remains so today. In essence, we are extrapolating from confounded data and often cannot be confident that we have identified the "active ingredients" in character education. A parallel interest would be in discovering which specific practices impact which specific character outcomes, another missing piece in this puzzle. Both of these gaps are further complicated by the fact that the only formal meta-analysis in the set of reviews is the Durlak et al. (2011) study, which was only part of the CASEL database and which did not systematically study specific strategies. Other reviews varied in their systematicity, but we had to use what was available. Currently we have begun a procedure for doing systematic reviews of the character education literature, in parallel to what is done in medical research. This is complex and expensive to do and we have been fortunate thus far to be funded by the Templeton, Bechtel and Singer foundations.

Our recent experience conducting collaborative and transparent systematic reviews has led us to the conclusion that real progress in the development of a rigorous and robust knowledge base for the field of character education would be greatly accelerated by philanthropic and government agency support for (1) individual studies of character strategies and programs as projects such as the Character Lab and PACE are doing (albeit with different approaches) but also (2) the development of a field building tool. We have conceptualized this as the "Character Development Systematic Review and Data Repository" (SRDR). The SRDR is an online tool for the systematic cataloging of scientific research that is searchable, public, expandable, and able to generate integrative conclusions about practice. A tool such as this would allow individual researchers and research teams from the various fields of research that now inform school-based character development to synergistically build the knowledge base in the way that medicine and healthcare have done. This would be accomplished through guided and filtered access for scientists to add to the database. The Center for Character and Citizenship has adapted, directly from the healthcare field, the SRDR at the Brown University Evidence-Based Practice Center. While having access to this technology is a huge step forward, it alone will not build a knowledge base. That requires the support and participation of a consortium of both funders and researchers. More of this type of research needs to be done to generate conclusions for which we can be more confident.

Nonetheless, this review offers a framework for choosing implementation strategies and designing a comprehensive initiative to promote the development of character and socioemotional competencies. Those engaging in such an endeavor would be well-served to clearly identify their outcome goals and then to select strategies from this report that align with those goals. In particular, taking a comprehensive approach which includes all of the six PRIMED principles and relying on strategies that have been identified in multiple reviews as effective practices would be a good strategy for those attempting to design and implement an effective character and socioemotional development initiative.

AUTHOR NOTE

Marvin W. Berkowitz, Center for Character and Citizenship, University of Missouri-St. Louis; Melinda C. Bier, Center for Character and Citizenship, University of Missouri-St. Louis; Brian McCauley, Center for Character and Citizenship, University of Missouri-St. Louis. Brian McCauley is now at Wasatch Academy, Utah. This work was supported by in part by grants from the John Templeton Foundation, the Steven Bechtel Jr. Foundation, and the Harry S. Singer Foundation

REFERENCES

Althof, W., & Berkowitz, M. W. (2006). Moral education and character education: Their relationship and their roles in citizenship education. *Journal of Moral Education, 35,* 495–518.

Beland, K. (2003). *Eleven principles sourcebook: How to achieve quality character education in K–12 schools.* Washington, DC: Character.org.

Benninga, J. S., Berkowitz, M. W., Kuehn, P., & Smith, K. (2003). The relationship of character education implementation and academic achievement in elementary schools. *Journal of Research in Character Education, 1,* 19–32.

Berger, R. (2003). *An ethic of excellence: Building a culture of craftsmanship with students.* Portsmouth, NH: Heinemann.

Berkowitz, M. W. (2009). Teaching in your PRIME. In D. Streight (Ed.), *Good things to do: Expert suggestions for fostering goodness in kids* (pp. 9–14). Portland, OR: Council for Spiritual and Ethical Education Publications.

Berkowitz, M. W. (2011a). What works in values education. *International Journal of Educational Research, 50,* 153–158.

Berkowitz, M. W. (2011b). Leading schools of character. In A. M. Blankstein & P. D. Houston (Eds.), *The soul of educational leadership series: Vol. 9. Leadership for social justice and democracy in our schools* (pp. 93–121). Thousand Oaks, CA: Corwin.

Berkowitz, M. W. (2012). *You can't teach through a rat: And other epiphanies for educators.* Chapel Hill, NC: Character Development.

Berkowitz, M. W., Althof, W., & Bier, M. C. (2012). The practice of pro-social education. In P. Brown, M. Corrigan, & A. Higgins-D'Alessandro (Eds.), *The handbook of prosocial education* (Vol. 1, pp. 71–90). Lanham MD: Rowman & Littlefield.

Berkowitz, M. W., & Bier, M. C. (2005). *What works in character education: A research-driven guide for educators.* Washington, DC: Character Education Partnership.

Berkowitz, M. W., & Bier, M.C. (2007). What works in character education. *Journal of Research in Character Education, 5,* 29–48.

Berkowitz, M. W., & Bier, M. C. (2014). Research-based fundamentals of the effective promotion of character development in schools. In L. Nucci, D. Narvaez, & T. Krettenauer (Eds.), *Handbook on moral and character education* (pp. 248–260). New York, NY: Routledge.

Berkowitz, M. W., & Bustamante, A. (2013). Using research to set priorities for character education in schools: A global perspective. *Korean Journal of Educational Policy, 2013,* 7–20.

Berkowitz, M. W., & Grych, J. (1998). Fostering goodness: Teaching parents to facilitate children's moral development. *Journal of Moral Education, 27,* 371–391.

Berkowitz, M. W., & Grych, J. H. (2000). Early character development and education. *Early Education and Development, 11,* 55–72.

Berkowitz, M. W., Pelster, K., & Johnston, A. (2012). Leading in the middle: A tale of pro-social education reform in two principals and two middle schools. In P. Brown, M. Corrigan, & A. Higgins-D'Alessandro (Eds.), *The handbook of prosocial education* (Vol. 2, pp. 619–626). Lanham, MD: Rowman & Littlefield.

Billig, S. H. (2002). Support for K–12 service-learning practice: A brief review of the research. *Educational Horizons, Summer,* 184–189.

Bryk, A., & Schneider, B. L. (2002). *Trust in schools: A core resource for improvement.* New York, NY: Russel Sage Foundation.

CASEL (2005). *Safe and sound: An educational leader's guide to evidence-based Social and Emotional (SEL) programs.* Chicago IL: Collaborative for Academic Social and Emotional Learning.

CASEL. (2015). *CASEL Guide: Effective social and emotional learning programs: Middle and high school edition.* Retrieved from http://Secondaryguide.casel.org

Damon, W. (2008). *The path to purpose: How young people find their calling in life.* New York, NY: Free Press.

Darling-Hammond, L. (2002). *Re-designing high schools: What matters and what works.* Stanford CA: Stanford Redesign Network.

Davidson, M., Lickona, T., & Khmelkov, V. (2008). Smart and good schools: A new paradigm for high school character education. In L. Nucci & D. Narvaez (Eds.), *Handbook on moral and character education* (pp. 1–28). New York, NY: Routledge.

Deci, E. L., Koestner, R., & Ryan, R. M. (1999). A meta-analytic review of experiments examining the effects of extrinsic rewards on intrinsic motivation. *Psychological Bulletin, 125,* 627–668.

Deci, E. L., & Ryan, R. M. (2002). *An overview of self-determination theory handbook of self determination research.* Rochester, NY: University of Rochester Press.

Duckworth, A. (2016). *GRIT: The power of passion and perseverance.* New York, NY: Scribner.

Duckworth, A. L., Grant, H., Loew, B., Oettingen, G., & Gollwitzer, P. M. (2011). Self-regulation strategies improve self-discipline in adolescents: Benefits of mental contrasting and implementation intentions. *Educational Psychology: An International Journal of Experimental Educational Psychology, 31,* 17–26.

Durlak, J. A., Weissberg, R. P., Dymnicki, A. B., Taylor, R. D., & Schellinger, K. B. (2011). The impact of enhancing students' social and emotional learning: A meta-analysis of school-based universal interventions. *Child Development, 82,* 405–432.

Frugo, J., Johnston, A., McCauley, B., & Navarro, K. (2016). *Leading character: A collaborative investigation into the characteristics and strategies of effective character education leaders.* Unpublished paper, University of Missouri-St. Louis.

Gollwitzer, P. M. (1999). Implementation intentions. Strong effects of simple plans. *American Psychologist, 54,* 493–503.

Hattie, J. (2009). *Visible learning: A synthesis of over 800 meta-analyses relating to achievement.* New York, NY: Routledge.

Hattie, J., & Yates, G. (2014). *Visible learning and the science of how we learn.* New York, NY: Routledge.

Heckman, J. J., & Kautz, T. (2014). Fostering and measuring skills: Interventions that improve character and cognition. In J. J. Heckman, J. E. Humphries, & T. Kautz (Eds.), *The myth of achievement tests: The GED and the role of character in American life* (pp. 341–430). Chicago, IL: University of Chicago Press.

Johnson, D. W., & Johnson, R. T. (1987). *Learning together and alone: cooperative, competitive, and individualistic learning.* Upper Saddle River, NJ: Prentice-Hall.

Johnston, A. (2012). Case Study 6A: Francis Howell Middle School, Missouri. In P. Brown, M. Corrigan, & A. Higgins-D'Alessandro (Eds.), *The handbook of prosocial education* (Vol. 1, pp. 137–142). Lanham, MD: Rowman & Littlefield.

Leithwood, K., Harris, A., & Hopkins, D. (2008). Seven strong claims about successful school leadership. *Leadership & Management, 28,* 27–42.

Leming, J. S. (1997). Research and practice in character education: A historical perspective. In A. Molnar (Ed.), *The construction of children's character: 86th yearbook of the National Society for the Study of Education, Part 2* (pp. 31–44). Chicago, IL: The National Society for the Study of Education.

Lickona, T. (1991). *Educating for character: How our schools can teach respect and responsibility.* New York, NY: Bantam.

Lickona, T. (2004). *Character matters: How to help our children develop good judgment, integrity, and other essential virtues.* New York, NY: Simon & Schuster.

Lickona, T., & Davidson, M. (2005). *Smart and good high schools: Integrating excellence and ethics for success in school, work, and beyond.* Washington, DC: Character.org.

Lovat, T., Toomey, R., Dally, K., & Clement, N. (2009). *Project to test and measure the impact of values education on student effects and school ambience* (Final Report for Australian Government, Department of Education, Employment and Workplace Relations).

Marshall, J. C., Caldwell, S. D., & Foster, J. (2011). Moral education the CHARACTER*plus* way. *Journal of Moral Education, 40,* 51–72.

Marzano, R. J. (2003). *What works in schools: Translating research into action.* Alexandria VA: ASCD.

Marzano, R. J., Waters, T., & McNulty, B. A. (2001). *School leadership that works: From research to results.* New York, NY: Barnes & Noble.

Oettingen, G. (2000). Expectancy effects on behavior depend on self-regulatory thought. *Social Cognition, 18,* 101–129.

Oettingen, G., & Gollwitzer, P. M. (2009). Making goal pursuit effective: Expectancy-dependent goal setting and planned goal striving. In J. P. Forgas, R. F. Baumeister, & D. M. Tice (Eds.), *Psychology of self-regulation: Cognitive, affective, and motivational processes* (pp. 127–146). New York, NY: Psychology Press.

Public Profit. (2014). Strategies to promote non-cognitive skills: A guide for youth development and educators. Retrieved from http://www.publicprofit.net/Strategies-To-Promote-Non-Cognitive-Skills

Reeve, J. M., & Halusic, M. (2009). How K–12 teachers can put self-determination theory principles into practice. *Theory and Research in Education, 7,* 145–154.

Ryan, R. M., & Deci, E. L. (2013). Toward a social psychology of assimilation: Self-determination theory in cognitive development and education. In B. W. Sokol, F. M. E. Grouzet, U. Muller (Eds.), *Self-regulation and autonomy: Social and developmental dimensions of human conduct* (pp. 191–207). Cambridge, England: Cambridge University Press.

Shields, D. L. (2011, May). Character as the aim of education. *Phi Delta Kappan, 92,* 48–53.

Streight, D. (2015). *Breaking into the heart of character: Self-determined moral action and academic motivation* (3rd ed.). Washington, DC: Centers for Spiritual and Ethical Education.

Thapa, A., Cohen, J., Higgins-D'Alessandro, & Guffey, S. (2012). *School climate research summary.* New York, NY: National School Climate Center. Retrieved from www.schoolclimate.org/climate/documents/policy/sc-brief-v3.pdf

Tough, P. (2012). *How children succeed: Grit, curiosity, and the hidden power of character.* New York, NY: Houghton Mifflin Harcourt.

Urban, H. (2008). *Lessons from the classroom: 20 things good teachers do.* Redwood CA: Great Lessons Press.

Urban, J. B., Hargraves, M., & Trochim, W. M. (2014). Evolutionary evaluation: Implications for evaluators, researchers, practitioners, funders and the evidence-based program mandate. *Evaluation and Program Planning, 45,* 127–139.

U.S. Department of Education. (2013). *Promoting grit, tenacity, and perseverance: Critical factors for success in the 21st century.* Washington, DC: U.S. Department of Education Office of Educational Technology.

Watson, M. (2003). *Learning to trust: Transforming difficult elementary classrooms through developmental discipline.* San Francisco, CA: Jossey-Bass.

Wentzel, K. R. (2002). Are effective teachers like parents? Teaching styles and student adjustment in early adolescence. *Child Development, 73,* 287–301.

Yeager, D. S., & Walton, G. M. (2011). Social-psychological interventions in education: They're not magic. *Review of Educational Research, 81,* 267–301.

ILLUMINATING THE MECHANISMS OF CHARACTER DEVELOPMENT

Camille A. Farrington
University of Chicago, Consortium on School Research

This paper responds to Berkowitz, Bier, and McCauley's description of effective features and practices that support character development by pushing on the question of *how* child and youth environments might "build character." Acknowledging the challenges of drawing on program evaluations and extant studies of character development to identify promising practices, the author suggests a more thorough leveraging of both theoretical work and empirical studies in other disciplines (e.g., neuroscience, cognitive science, social psychology, developmental psychology, sociology, philosophy) to theorize about potential mechanisms whereby school practices develop character in children and adolescents. Utilizing a recent developmental framework, the Foundations for Young Adult Success (Nagaoka, Farrington, Ehrlich, & Heath, 2015), the author proposes that 10 particular "developmental experiences"—specific opportunities provided for young people to act and reflect—are key mechanisms whereby settings influence the development of character and equip children and youth to build toward agency, an integrated identity, and a set of competencies that support success in young adulthood.[1] These developmental experiences are briefly summarized and some potential alignments with Berkowitz and colleagues' PRIMED framework are noted.

Berkowitz, Bier, and MacAuley (this issue) remind us that the ultimate goal of character education "is for children and adolescents to become good people, to develop into and act as agents for good in the world. [It] is about *being* people of character even more than it is about *acting* good" (p. 43). Over the past decade, Berkowitz and colleagues have periodically reviewed empirical studies to better understand how schools can help to develop young people of character. By examining the effects of specific strategies on character development, they have identified common strategies across effective programs (Berkowitz, 2011; Berkowitz & Bier, 2005, 2007, 2014). In this special issue they extend that work to include results from a recent review of reviews.

Taken together, this body of work represents a significant contribution to research and practice in character education. However, in reviewing the empirical literature, Berkowitz et al. are limited by the research methodologies utilized in the studies they reviewed and the quality and scope of the data those methods

• **Correspondence concerning this article should be addressed to:** Camille A. Farrington, camillef@uchicago.edu

Journal of Character Education, Volume 13(1), 2017, pp. 53–65
Copyright © 2017 Information Age Publishing, Inc.

produced. They have done a laudable job of elevating key strategies associated with effective practice in character education, but more work needs to be done to illuminate the *mechanisms* whereby good practice develops the character of children and adolescents in K–12 schools and to further build robust theory about character development.

Berkowitz and colleagues (2017) pursued three approaches to identifying evidence-based practices for developing character from the available empirical literature. Where studies identified specific practices with evidence of effects, they were able to link practices to the character outcomes those practices produced. Where studies evaluated programs whole cloth, they attempted to deconstruct the programs to identify specific practices or strategies within them as well as the kinds of impacts associated with the programs. Finally, in some cases they worked backward from specific outcomes to see what research or theory said about potential causal factors. The central challenge across these three approaches, as they noted, was that very few studies identified both specific practices and specific outcomes that could be causally linked by the available evidence.

The methodological challenges of research to determine "effectiveness" of character education are enormous. Human development is a complex, multidimensional, nonlinear process that occurs across a variety of settings over a long period of time; as such, it does not lend itself well to random assignment or controlled trials. Collecting compelling and unambiguous outcome data is particularly challenging. Consider Berkowitz et al.'s (2017) broad definition of character as "the set of psychological characteristics that motivate and enable one to function as a moral agent, to perform optimally, to effectively pursue knowledge and intellectual flourishing, and to be an effective member of society." By this definition, there are at least four discrete outcomes of character development (moral, performance, intellectual, and civic); being able to tie particular strategies to varied and specific character

outcomes is seldom possible with the still-too-crude tools available to social scientists. Further, few studies follow students for a long enough time period to really understand long-term developmental outcomes. Researchers must often rely on discrete behaviors or other short-term outcomes as proxies for "being a person of good character" or of developing toward becoming one. But getting students to turn in homework at higher rates or to learn helpful steps for calming down when angry is no guarantee that they are in fact developing good character that will endure.

The input side of the research equation is equally challenging. As Berkowitz and colleagues noted, most of the existing research evaluates holistic programs, with few studies identifying specific practices or strategies, let alone testing their effects. Even where specific program components are described, it is impossible to isolate the impact of one component versus another.

Complicating this even further is the fact that development is dependent not only on what the inputs are, but on what individual children make of those inputs, how they interpret them, and how they make meaning of them. Character development, as all aspects of human development, is as much a phenomenological process as a neurological or behavioral one. Adults employ various practices, strategies, rules, and guidelines in raising and educating children, hoping that they grow up to be good and learned people, but one can never be certain in the moment that these methods will bear fruit. Researchers could study such processes exhaustively, and still not hope to isolate exactly which variables at what dosages and durations and in what order will ensure goodness and kindness and steadfastness in adulthood. And yet, study we do, from a wide variety of disciplinary lenses. Perhaps it is by taking a broad, multidisciplinary view that we can best decipher the big picture of character development emerging from the research.

Based on the current state of the field, Berkowitz, Bier, and MacAuley make two recommendations for future work. One is a call for coordinated investment in targeted studies of specific strategies and practices aimed at developing young people's character and socioemotional competencies. The second is a field-building tool in the form of an interactive data repository as researchers collectively accumulate more evidence of effective practices. While these both seem like worthy and important efforts, I would suggest an additional approach. A major shortcoming of reviewing program evaluations and studies of extant strategies is that this approach results in a listing of prevalent practices that is largely atheoretical. While the reviews and resulting PRIMED framework developed by Berkowitz and colleagues have contributed significantly to illustrating examples of effective practice in character education, they have done less to advance broader theory or to illuminate the specific mechanisms that make these practices "effective." How does prioritizing character education or empowering stakeholders turn into young people with good character?

In addition to the work that Berkowitz, Bier, and MacAuley have undertaken and the recommendations they make for future study, I advocate for drawing on the extensive theoretical and empirical literature on learning and development to build theory about *why* specific school practices might lead to positive character outcomes. For example, what do neurological studies or psychological interventions with young people suggest about strategies that build neural pathways associated with emotional competence, that support moral reasoning, or that reinforce positive behavioral habits? Leveraging the broader literature on learning and development seems like a fruitful avenue for building robust theory of effective character education and illuminating the mechanisms of character development in young people.

Unfortunately, expanding theory and knowledge about developmental mechanisms doesn't solve the many challenges associated with studying outcomes of youth development. Theorized mechanisms can be investigated empirically using observation tools for detecting their presence in schools and other youth settings, and utilizing available science to measure specific short-run student-level outcomes believed to be fostered by these mechanisms (e.g., empathy, social problem-solving skills, sense of belonging, civic participation, school attendance), checking for hypothesized associations. Ultimately, the effects of identified mechanisms can be rigorously tested through randomized controlled trials where such mechanisms are added into existing youth programs or educational settings and compared with previous practice. Still, by drawing from evidence across disciplines, we can contribute to the field of youth development research and practice by hypothesizing mechanisms whereby development happens.

THE FOUNDATIONS FOR YOUNG ADULT SUCCESS: A DEVELOPMENTAL FRAMEWORK

As applied education researchers who study youth development with a particular eye toward practice, my colleagues and I at the University of Chicago Consortium on School Research have taken up the question of how young people both *learn* and *become*, across the myriad settings in which they act and grow (Farrington et al., 2012; Nagaoka et al., 2015). Our most recent work has led us to identify a set of ten "developmental experiences" that the research suggests are associated with both neurological (building neural pathways) and phenomenological (making meaning of one's experience) aspects of character development. This work contributes to the field of character education by hypothesizing specific mechanisms of development, pushing researchers and practitioners to think about not only the types of adult practices associated with student character outcomes, but also the kinds of character-building experiences and opportunities that young people are afforded across school, home, and community. Ultimately, it is what children and youth *do* and *experience*—and the *meaning* they make of those experiences—that lead to young people's development.

In 2013, my colleagues and I were commissioned by the Wallace Foundation to (1) identify key factors contributing to young adult success, (2) study how those factors developed over time, and (3) note the implications for practice in school, home, and community settings. Our methods included in-depth review of the empirical literature and expert interviews with researchers, practitioners, and policymakers. We worked across disciplines in education, child/youth development, social psychology, sociology, neuroscience, economics, cognitive sciences, and philosophy (Nagaoka et al., 2015).

From our investigation, we created a framework of the Foundations for Young Adult Success (FYAS), depicted by a double-ringed graphic illustration (see Figure 1) of the essential ingredients for success in young adulthood across a variety of domains (education, work, relationships, civic engagement) (Nagaoka et al., 2015). The outer ring of the Foundations for Young Adult Success framework consists of three *key factors*: **agency**, **integrated identity**, and **competencies**. We conceptualize these key factors as what parents, teachers, and other youth developers might hold as a North Star in the raising, teaching, and mentoring of children and adolescents: young adults who are able to navigate constraints, make choices about, and act on behalf of themselves and their communities (**agency**); who are self-aware and able to integrate their various strengths and social identities in a way that provides them with a solid and expansive foundation (**integrated identity**); and who have a set of socially valued interpersonal, academic, and technical competencies that allow them to be productive and contributing members of their families, communities, workplaces, and civic institutions (**competencies**).

The inner ring of the Foundations for Young Adult Success framework shows four *foundational components*, mutually reinforcing elements that underlie and enable the three key factors (Nagaoka et al., 2015). **Self-regulation** encompasses executive function skills and the general awareness of and ability to direct one's behaviors, thoughts, and emotions (Bandura, 1991; Baumeister, Heatherton, & Tice, 1994). **Knowledge and skills** denotes what one knows and can do across a variety of domains (academic, interpersonal, technical, cultural, institutional). These become the constituent parts from which broader competencies are built.[2] **Mindsets** are attitudes and beliefs about oneself and the world; mindsets of openness, self-efficacy, belongingness, and the malleability of intelligence (growth mindset) have been shown to support positive action and improved performance in a variety of settings (Bandura, 1993; Dweck, 2006; Farrington et al., 2012; McCrae & Sutin, 2009; Walton, & Cohen, 2011). **Values** are the fourth foundational component, lasting beliefs about what is good, bad, and important in life that act as a moral code of conduct to guide behavior, enduring preferences, and one's larger sense of purpose (Rokeach, 1973; Schwartz, 1992). These four foundational components work together to shape and inform human choice and behavior and ultimately enable the key factors of agency, integrated identity, and competencies in adulthood. Table 1, taken from our original report, further defines each of these factors and components in the Foundations for Young Adult Success framework. In Nagaoka et al. (2015), we show the developmental progression of each of these foundational components across five developmental stages from early childhood through young adulthood.

A central question in our study focused on *how* the key factors and foundational components identified in the Foundations for Young Adult Success framework develop over time. As Berkowitz and colleagues point out, schools often focus on strategies to shape students' behavior, but they "are not equally effective in nurturing the development of people" (Berkowitz, Bier, & MacAuley, this issue, p. 43). To influence children's long-term development, it is insufficient to focus solely on inputs, conditions, and strategies. To best

Source: Nagaoka et al. (2015, p. 20).

FIGURE 1
FYAS Framework: Key Factors and Foundational Components

leverage settings and adult practices to maximize youth learning and development, we have to understand something about the underlying mechanisms whereby these inputs, conditions, and strategies result in "character."

Developmental Experiences

Emerging from our review of evidence, a set of 10 "developmental experiences" was identified—five action experiences and five reflection experiences—that appear in the literature as critical mechanisms for transforming children's daily experience into learning and becoming—and for developing a set of navigational tools grounded in both knowledge and wisdom, an adaptive orientation toward life, and the habitual good behaviors associated with "character." Developmental experiences are defined here as activities that provide children and youth with the necessary conditions and stimuli to advance their development as appropriate to their age. I build upon Larson, Hansen, & Moneta's (2006) concept of developmental experiences to identify opportunities for specific types of action and reflection that the literature suggests are the means through which young people build specific capacities and competencies. The developmental experiences model presented here

TABLE 1

Definitions of Key Factors and Foundational Components of Young Adult Success

Key Factors		
These three factors support a successful transition into young adulthood and capture how one interacts with the world, sees and understands oneself, and is able to apply one's capabilities to effect change.		
Agency is the ability to make choices about and take an active role in one's life path, rather than solely being the product of one's circumstances. Agency requires the intentionality and forethought to derive a course of action and adjust course as needed to reflect one's identity, competencies, knowledge and skills, mindsets, and values.	**Integrated Identity** is a sense of internal consistency of who one is across time and across multiple social identities (e.g., race/ethnicity, profession, culture, gender, religion). An integrated identity serves as an internal framework for making choices and provides a stable base from which one can act in the world.	**Competencies** are the abilities that enable people to effectively perform roles, complete complex tasks, or achieve specific objectives. Successful young adults have sets of competencies (e.g., critical thinking, responsible decision-making, collaboration) that allow them to be productive and engaged, navigate across contexts, perform effectively in different settings, and adapt to different task and setting demands.

Foundational Components			
These are a set of cognitive and noncognitive components that underlie the three key factors. Each of the four components directly fosters learning and growth, while also reinforcing and enhancing the other foundational components. Each component and subcomponent has corollaries that apply to self, others, or the world.			
Self-Regulation is a set of internal processes that enable one to manage one's behavior, emotions, attention, and cognition while engaging with the world toward a goal. Self-regulation has numerous forms, including cognitive, emotional, behavioral, and attentional regulation. Literature suggests that there are two aspects of self-regulation that support successful interactions with others and the world: *self-control*, which is cognitively controlled by executive function skills, and *awareness*—of oneself, other people, and one's surroundings.	**Knowledge** is sets of facts, information, or understanding about oneself, others, and the world. **Skills** are the learned abilities to carry out a task with intended results or goals. Skills can be general or domain specific, and can be academic, technical, professional, cultural, or institutional in nature. **Knowledge and Skills** are developed over a lifetime, and individuals draw on them in everyday experiences, which help sustain other foundational components and build key factors.	**Mindsets** are beliefs and attitudes about oneself, the external world, and the interaction between the two. They are the default lenses that individuals use to process everyday experiences. Mindsets reflect a person's unconscious biases, natural tendencies, and past experiences. Though mindsets are malleable, they tend to persist until disrupted and replaced with a different belief or attitude.	**Values** are ideals or beliefs about what is good or bad and what is desirable or undesirable. They are important, enduring, and often culturally defined. Values develop through a process of exploration and experimentation, where young people make sense of their experiences and refine what they hold as important ideals. Values serve as broad guidelines for roles and relationships, and provide an orientation for one's desired future.

Source: Nagaoka et al. (2015, p. 29).

draws from theoretical and empirical evidence that cuts across different disciplinary perspectives and theories of learning. Across this wide base of research, particular kinds of action and reflection experiences were repeatedly implicated as critical components of how learning happens. These developmental experiences are largely consistent, and in some cases overlapping, with the guiding principles in Berkowitz et al.'s PRIMED framework (Berkowitz, 2009; Berkowitz & Bier, 2014; Berkowitz & Busta-

mante, 2013; Burkowitz et al., 2017), but they shift the focus from contextual inputs or adult practices to what young people *do* and how they *make meaning* within those inputs and practices.

I argue here, in short, that youth become "good people" through developmental experiences that build their capacity to regulate their behavior, develop their understanding of the world, cultivate attitudes and beliefs that support their growth, and develop a set of values

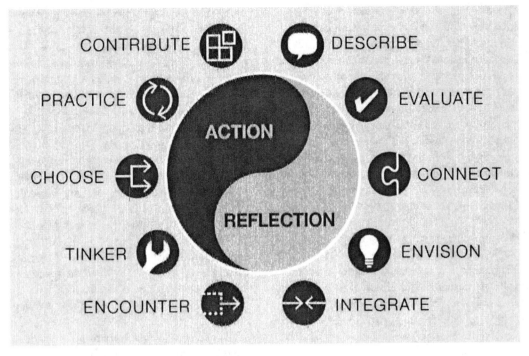

Source: Nagaoka et al. (2015, p. 39).

FIGURE 2
Developmental Experiences Wheel

and a moral vision that can guide their decisions and actions. In this way, the concept of developmental experiences builds upon earlier theories of positive youth development that emphasized "developmental assets" as building blocks to healthy growth and development (Benson, Scales, Hamilton, & Sesma, 2006). Importantly, as is called out by Berkowitz and other youth development scholars, these developmental experiences are most powerful in the context of strong, supportive, and sustained developmental relationships with caring adults (Berkowitz et al., 2017; Li & Julian, 2012; Scales, Benson, & Roehlkepartain, 2011).

I focus here on broad lines of work that depict learning as *experiential* and *social,* as well as work that examines the underlying *neurological* components of learning. Though there is still perhaps far more we don't understand about learning and development than we

do, together these bodies of research suggest compelling courses of action for adults working with children and youth. This work is very briefly summarized here. For a fuller description of the evidence behind each developmental experience, see Nagaoka et al. (2015).

A long tradition of work in philosophy, psychology, and education emphasizes the critical role of experience in learning (Dewey, 1938/ 1969; Freire, 1970/1993; James, 1912; Kolb, 1984; Mezirow, 1985, 2000). Educational theorist David Kolb defined learning as "the process whereby knowledge is created through the transformation of experience" (1984, p. 41). This kind of direct experience—"the concrete, tangible, felt qualities of the world, relying on our senses, and immersing ourselves in concrete reality"—is one of the primary ways children perceive new information (Kolb, p. 41). But certain types of experiences provide richer opportunities for development than others. Rich developmental experiences include those that put children in interaction with others (peers and adults); build strong and supportive relationships; and provide opportunities to play and explore, try on new roles and perspectives, publicly demonstrate new skills and competencies, and contribute to endeavors that are personally and socially meaningful.

Drawing from extensive research on how children learn and how habits are developed (e.g., Bransford, Brown, & Cocking, 2000; Ericsson & Charness, 1994; Lally, Van Jaarsveld, Potts, & Wardle, 2010), the developmental experiences model includes both *active* and *reflective* components. The *active* component of developmental experiences provides opportunities for children and youth to *encounter, tinker, practice, choose, and contribute.* **Encountering** involves exposure to a variety of people, perspectives, roles, and places. This includes opportunities to watch others and have access to models or exemplars. Encountering new ways of thinking and being and models of advanced practice are some of the primary ways youth take in information about the world and expand their sense of possibility (Halpern, Heckman, & Larson, 2013; Kolb, 1984; Vygotsky, 1978). The literature in this area suggests why the principle of modeling in the PRIMED framework may be important to character development, as well as to the critical role of mentors and role models noted in the principle of Relationships.

Tinkering involves extended and uninterrupted periods of time for children to explore their environments. Developing an understanding of how the world works requires opportunities to play around, take things apart, or try various solutions in a low-risk, low-stakes setting. Tinkering includes imaginative play in early childhood and experimenting with new personas in adolescence, both essential preparation for successfully taking on adult roles (Hughes, 1999; Schwartz, Coté, Arnett, 2005; Singer, Golinkoff, & Hirsh-Pasek, 2006; Weisberg & Gopnik, 2013). The research supporting tinkering as a

developmental experience aligns with implementation strategies in the PRIMED framework, including the importance of a "safe environment" (Prioritization principle, subcategory of climate) and of "Opportunities for revising one's work/efforts" (Intrinsic Motivation principle, subcategory of self-growth).

Practicing extends upon encountering and tinkering by providing the opportunity to build skills and competencies over time. There is strong empirical support for practice as a major factor in developing expertise (Bengtsson et al., 2005; Ericsson & Charness, 1994; Ericsson, Krampe, & Tesch-Römer, 1993; Winstein, 2014) as well as motivation for continued learning. Ultimately, practice prepares children and youth to be successful in future performance. The research literature on practicing lends support for Berkowitz and colleagues' inclusion of "Practice" as a subcategory in the PRIMED framework and "role playing/practice" as an effective strategy under the Developmental Pedagogy principle.

Choosing fulfills children's and youth's basic psychological needs for autonomy (Deci & Ryan, 1985; Ryan & Deci, 2000), supports young people to feel in control of their own destinies, and fosters cognitive, moral, and social development (Assor, 2012; Erikson, 1950/1963; Stefanou, Perencevich, DiCintio, & Turner, 2004). Providing meaningful choices motivates further participation, setting up a positive developmental cycle (Zuckerman, Porac, Lathin, Smith, & Deci, 1978). The research on choosing provides further support for the principle of "Empowerment" in the PRIMED framework, as the practices of "shared leadership" and "democratic classrooms" provide opportunities for students to make meaningful choices.

Finally, **contributing** provides young people with opportunities to solve problems or bring into the world works of value to the self and others. Contributing is called out in several youth development models (Pittman, Irby, & Ferber, 2010; Zeldin, 1995), and cited as the "Sixth C" of positive youth development (Lerner, 2004).[3] Contributing is important not only because of its altruistic aspects and its value to a community; making meaningful contributions that are valued by others also builds young people's self-confidence and sense of competence (Hattie & Yates, 2014). For adolescents, opportunities to contribute help to integrate the moral and civic (and perhaps spiritual) components of identity and instill an ethic of giving back (Damon, 2008; King & Benson, 2006). This aligns with and helps to explain the developmental importance of the practices of "Opportunities for moral action" and "Community service/service learning" (subcategory of Service) in the PRIMED framework (Intrinsic Motivation principle).

It is through experience that youth develop the foundational components for success. But if experience is to have lasting benefit, it must be infused with meaning and integrated into one's emerging sense of identity. Learning is accelerated and more readily transferred to other situations when one reflects on what happened, what worked, and what needs improving (Palincsar & Brown, 1984; Scardamalia, Bereiter, & Steinbach, 1984; Schoenfeld, 1983, 1985, 1991). The *reflective* component of developmental experiences provides opportunities for young people to make sense and meaning of their active participation by *describing* and *evaluating* their experiences and observations, *connecting* experiences to other things they care about, *envisioning* how an experience might inform or contribute to a desirable future, and, over time, *integrating* one's developmental experiences into one's self-concept and the "story" of oneself.

Describing and evaluating events and activities help children to "own" an experience and define it for themselves. Children build knowledge and vocabulary by talking about the world—and the more knowledge and vocabulary they build, the more able they are to participate in discussions about how things work (Huttenlocher, Waterfall, Vasilyeva, Vevea, & Hedges, 2010). For older youth, dialogue fosters close social relationships, helps youth figure out their values and perspectives,

and creates the conditions for making substantive change as they "name the world" for themselves (Freire, 1970/1993, p. 88). Throughout the PRIMED framework are opportunities for describing and evaluating, including the emphasis in Prioritization on using "common language" and "providing opportunities for [self-]assessment and feedback for character/SEL."

Connecting is a fundamental cognitive process; the human brain thinks in terms of *relationships*, guiding the storage and retrieval of information and ideas into and from long-term memory (Bransford et al., 2000; Hattie & Yates, 2014). Creating connections not only helps to build cognitive understanding, but it also allows youth to direct and maintain their attention. Tasks that are connected to something a student values increases their interest, persistence, and performance of the task (Damon, 2008; Wigfield & Eccles, 1992). The importance in the literature of connecting as a developmental mechanism suggests why fostering "empathy" and using a "challenging/meaningful/relevant curriculum" (Intrinsic Motivation principle) might be effective character education practices.

Envisioning is the act of imaging oneself in the future. Young people need opportunities to envision and construct concrete, positive futures for themselves that embrace their important social identities (Oyserman & James, 2011). This is particularly important where social stereotypes place limitations on the future expectations for marginalized subgroups (Espinoza-Herold, 2003; Oyserman & Fryberg, 2006). The literature on envisioning parallels the PRIMED framework's inclusion of "goal setting/imagining possible selves" in their list of effective practices.

Integrating refers to the act of incorporating insights, nascent skills, and other "life lessons" into one's larger sense of self in a way that expands a young person's competencies and agency in the world (Erikson, 1950/1963; Moshman, 2005). Adolescents especially need opportunities to author their own life narratives (McAdams & Adler, 2010), particularly if their social identity is one for whom the dominant narrative is limiting or negative (Perry, Steele, & Hilliard, 2003). Integration moves a young person from a stance of "I did that" to embrace a larger implication for one's identity: "I'm the kind of person who can...." Berkowitz and colleagues' inclusion of the "use of reflection (especially moral)" as an effective practice in the PRIMED framework (Intrinsic Motivation principle) is aligned with the evidence on integrating as a developmental mechanism.

In summary, developmental experiences are those which expose young people to new ideas, people, and perspectives, demonstrations of expert performance, and models of high quality work to emulate (*encounter*); provide opportunities to engage in hands-on learning (*tinker*); offer extended time to rehearse, role play, and develop competencies (*practice*); make consequential decisions about one's time, activities, and modes of expression (*choice*); and make meaningful contributions to causes beyond the self (*contribute*). In addition to these five action experiences, the literature points to five important reflection experiences. These include opportunities to "name the world" and assert one's perspective (*describe* and *evaluate*); draw parallels between new ideas and experiences and other things one cares about (*connections*); and imagine one's future life and self (*envision*). Finally, developmental experiences provide opportunities for young people to weave together their many social identities into a larger sense of themselves that can propel them forward (*integrate*). Developmental experiences thus set the stage for acting with agency in the world. Indeed, "when a concrete experience is enriched by reflection, given meaning by thinking, and transformed by action, the new experience created becomes richer, broader, and deeper" (Kolb & Kolb, 2009, p. 309).

Empirical evidence and rich theory suggest that these developmental experiences are important mechanisms by which character is developed. By augmenting studies of the effects of specific practices in character education with an equal attention to empirical and theoretical work about the mechanisms of character development, researchers can move the field substantially farther and make richer contributions to practice in schools, communities, and families.

NOTES

1. Invited paper for the National Academies of Sciences, Engineering, and Medicine Workshop on Defining and Measuring Character and Character Education, July 26–27, 2016. The developmental experiences theory highlighted in this paper was developed by the author through a project generously supported by The Wallace Foundation, originally published in *Foundations for Young Adult Success: A Developmental Framework* (Nagaoka et al., 2015), a report by the University of Chicago Consortium on School Research.
2. For example, being a competent voter draws on knowledge of the political process, knowledge about issues and candidates on the ballot, communication skills to engage in dialogue with others to come to a deeper understanding of these issues, critical thinking about the pros and cons of particular positions, knowledge about when and where to register and to vote, and self-management to ensure that one gets oneself to the polls.
3. The Five C's of positive youth development are competence, confidence, connection, character, and caring (Lerner, Fisher, & Weinberg, 2000).

REFERENCES

Assor, A. (2012). Allowing choice and nurturing an inner compass: Educational practices supporting students' need for autonomy. In S. L. Christenson, A. L. Reschly, & C. Wylie (Eds.), *Handbook of research on student engagement* (pp. 421–440). New York, NY: Springer.

Bandura, A. (1991). Social cognitive theory of self-regulation. *Organizational behavior and human decision processes, 50*(2), 248–287.

Bandura, A. (1993). Perceived self-efficacy in cognitive development and functioning. *Educational Psychologist, 28*(2), 117–148.

Baumeister, R. F., Heatherton, T. F., & Tice, D. M. (1994). *Losing control: How and why people fail at self-regulation.* San Diego, CA: Academic Press.

Bengtsson, S. L., Nagy, Z., Skare, S., Forsman, L., Forssberg, H., & Ullen, F. (2005). Extensive piano practicing has regionally specific effects on white matter development. *Nature Neuroscience, 8*(9), 1148–1150.

Benson P. L., Scales, P. C, Hamilton, S. F., & Sesma, A. (2006). Positive youth development: Theory, research, and applications. In R. M. Lerner (Ed.), *Theoretical models of human development: Vol. 1. Handbook of child psychology* (6th ed., pp. 894–941). Hoboken, NJ: Wiley.

Berkowitz, M. W. (2009). Teaching in your PRIME. In D. Streight (Ed.), *Good things to do: Expert suggestions for fostering goodness in kids* (pp. 9–14). Portland, OR: Council for Spiritual and Ethical Education Publications.

Berkowitz, M. W. (2011). What works in values education. *International Journal of Educational Research, 50,* 153–158.

Berkowitz, M. W., & Bier, M. C. (2005). *What works in character education: A research-driven guide for educators.* Washington, DC: Character Education Partnership.

Berkowitz, M. W., & Bier, M. C. (2007). What works in character education. *Journal of Research in Character Education, 5,* 29–48.

Berkowitz, M. W., & Bier, M. C. (2014). Research-based fundamentals of the effective promotion of character development in schools. In L. Nucci, D. Narvaez, & T. Krettenauer (Eds.), *Handbook on moral and character education* (pp. 248–260). New York, NY: Routledge.

Berkowitz, M. W., Bier, M. C., & MacAuley, B. (2017). Effective features and practices that support character development. *Journal of Character Education, 13*(1), 33–51.

Berkowitz, M. W., & Bustamante, A. (2013). Using research to set priorities for character education in schools: A global perspective. *Korean Journal of Educational Policy, 2013,* 7–20.

Bransford, J. D., Brown, A. L., & Cocking, R. R. (Eds.). (2000). *How people learn: Brain, mind, experience, and school. Expanded edition.* Washington, DC: National Academies Press.

Damon, W. (2008). *The path to purpose: Helping our children find their calling in life.* New York, NY: The Free Press.

Deci, E. L., & Ryan, R. M. (1985). *Intrinsic motivation and self-determination in human behavior.* New York, NY: Plenum Press.

Dewey, J. (1969). *Experience and education.* New York, NY: Collier. (Original work published 1938)

Dweck, C. S. (2006). *Mindset: The new psychology of success.* New York, NY: Random House.

Ericsson, K. A., & Charness, N. (1994). Expert performance: Its structure and acquisition. *American Psychological Association, 49*(8), 725–747.

Ericsson, K. A., Krampe, R. T., & Tesch-Römer, C. (1993). The role of deliberate practice in the acquisition of expert performance. *Psychological Review, 100*(3), 363–406.

Erikson, E. (1963). *Childhood and society* (2nd ed.). New York, NY: W. W. Norton & Co. (Original work published 1950)

Espinoza-Herold, M. (2003). *Issues in Latino education: Race, school culture, and the politics of academic success.* Boston, MA: Pearson Education Group.

Farrington, C. A., Roderick, M., Allensworth, E., Nagaoka, J., Keyes, T. S., Johnson, D. W., & Beechum, N. O. (2012). *Teaching adolescents to become learners—The role of noncognitive factors in shaping school performance: A critical literature review.* Chicago, IL: University of Chicago Consortium on School Research.

Freire, P. (1993). *Pedagogy of the oppressed.* London, England: Penguin Books. (Original work published 1970)

Halpern, R., Heckman, P. E., & Larson, R. W. (2013). *Realizing the potential of learning in middle adolescence.* West Hills, CA: The Sally and Dick Roberts Coyote Foundation.

Hattie, J., & Yates, G. (2014). *Visible learning and the science of how we learn.* New York, NY: Routledge.

Hughes, F. P. (1999). *Children, play, and development* (3rd ed.). Needham Heights, MA: Allyn & Bacon.

Huttenlocher, J., Waterfall, H., Vasilyeva, M., Vevea, J., & Hedges, L. V. (2010). Sources of variability in children's language growth. *Cognitive Psychology, 61,* 343–365.

James, W. (1912). *Essays in radical empiricism.* New York, NY: Longmans, Green.

King, P. E., & Benson, P. L. (2006). Spiritual development and adolescent well-being and thriving.

In E. C. Roehlkepartain, P. E. King, L. Wagener, & P. L. Benson (Eds.), *The handbook of spiritual development in childhood and adolescence* (pp. 384–398). Thousand Oaks, CA: SAGE.

Kolb, D. (1984). *Experiential learning: Experience as a source of learning and development.* Upper Saddle River, NJ: Prentice Hall.

Kolb, A. Y., & Kolb, D. A. (2009). The learning way: Meta-cognition aspects of experiential learning. *Simulation Gaming, 40*(3), 297–327.

Lally, P., Van Jaarsveld, C. H. M., Potts, H. W. W., & Wardle, J. (2010). How are habits formed: Modelling habit formation in the real world. *European Journal of Social Psychology, 40,* 998–1009.

Larson, R. W., Hansen, D. M., & Moneta, G. (2006). Differing profiles of developmental experiences across types of organized youth activities. *Developmental Psychology, 42*(5), 849–863.

Lerner R. M. (2004). *Liberty: Thriving and civic engagement among American youth.* Thousand Oaks, CA: SAGE.

Lerner, R. M., Fisher, C. B., & Weinberg, R. A. (2000). Toward a science for and of the people: Promoting civil society through the application of developmental science. *Child Development, 71*(1), 11–20.

Li, J., & Julian, M. M. (2012). Developmental relationships as the active ingredient: A unifying working hypothesis of "what works" across intervention settings. *American Journal of Orthopsychiatry, 82*(2), 157–166.

McAdams, D. P., & Adler, J. M. (2010). Autobiographical memory and the construction of a narrative identity: Theory, research, and clinical implications. In J. E. Maddux & J. Tangey (Eds.), *Social psychological foundations of clinical psychology* (pp. 36–50). New York, NY: Guilford Press.

McCrae, R. R., & Sutin, A. R. (2009). *Openness to experience.* New York, NY: Guilford Press.

Mezirow, J. (1985). A critical theory of self-directed learning. In S. Brookfield (Ed.), *New directions for adult and continuing education* (pp. 17–30). San Francisco, CA: Jossey-Bass.

Mezirow, J. (2000). Learning to think like an adult: Core concepts of transformation theory. In J. Mezirow & Associates (Eds.), *Learning as transformation: Critical perspectives on a theory in progress* (pp. 3–34). San Francisco, CA: Jossey-Bass.

Moshman, D. (2005). *Adolescent psychological development: Rationality, morality, and identity,* (2nd ed.). Mahwah, NJ: Erlbaum.

Nagaoka, J., Farrington, C. A., Ehrlich, S. B., & Heath, R. D. (2015). *Foundations for young adult success: A developmental framework.* Chicago, IL: University of Chicago Consortium on School Research.

Oyserman, D., & Fryberg, S. A. (2006). The possible selves of diverse adolescents: Content and function across gender, race, and national origin. In C. Dunkel & J. Kerpelman (Eds.), *Possible selves: Theory, research, and application* (pp. 17–39). Huntington, NY: Nova.

Oyserman, D., & James, L. (2011). Possible identities. In S. Schwartz, K. Luyckx, & V. Vignoles (Eds.), *Handbook of identity theory and research* (pp. 117–145). New York, NY: Springer.

Palincsar, A., & Brown, A. (1984). Reciprocal teaching of comprehension-fostering and comprehension-monitoring activities. *Cognition and Instruction, 1,* 117–175.

Perry, T., Steele, C., & Hilliard, A., III. (2003). *Young, gifted, and Black: Promoting high achievement among African American students.* Boston, MA: Beacon Press.

Pittman, K., Irby, M., & Ferber, T. (2001). Unfinished business: Further reflections on a decade of promoting youth development. In Public/Private Ventures (Ed.), *Youth development: Issues, challenges, and directions* (pp. 17–64). Philadelphia, PA: Public/Private Ventures.

Rokeach, M. (1973). *The nature of human values.* New York, NY: Free Press.

Ryan, R. M., & Deci, E. L. (2000). Intrinsic and extrinsic motivations: Classic definitions and new directions. *Contemporary educational psychology, 25*(1), 54–67.

Scales, P. C., Benson, P. L., & Roehlkepartain, E. C. (2011). Adolescent thriving: The role of sparks, relationships, and empowerment. *Journal of Youth and Adolescence, 40*(3), 263–277.

Scardamalia, M., Bereiter, C., & Steinbach, R. (1984). Teachability of reflective processes in written composition. *Cognitive Science, 8,* 173–190.

Schoenfeld, A. H. (1983). Problem solving in the mathematics curriculum: A report, recommendation, and an annotated bibliography. *Mathematical Association of American Notes,* No. 1.

Schoenfeld, A. H. (1985). *Mathematical problem solving.* Orlando, FL: Academic Press.

Schoenfeld, A. H. (1991). On mathematics as sense-making: An informal attack on the unfortunate divorce of formal and informal mathematics. In J. F. Voss, D. N. Perkins, & J. W. Segal (Eds.), *Informal reasoning and education* (pp. 311–343). Hillsdale, NJ: Erlbaum.

Schwartz, S. H. (1992). Universals in the content and structure of values: Theoretical advances and empirical tests in 20 countries. *Advances in experimental social psychology, 25,* 1–65.

Schwartz, S. J., Coté, J. E., & Arnett, J. J. (2005). Identity and agency in emerging adulthood: Two developmental routes in the individualization process. *Youth & Society, 37*(2), 201–229.

Singer, D., Golinkoff, R. M., & Hirsh-Pasek, K. (Eds.) (2006). *Play = learning: How play motivates and enhances children's cognitive and social-emotional growth.* New York, NY: Oxford University Press.

Stefanou, C. R., Perencevich, K. C., DiCintio, M., & Turner, J. C. (2004). Supporting autonomy in the classroom: Ways teachers encourage student decision making and ownership. *Educational Psychologist, 39*(4), 97–110.

Vygotsky, L. (1978). *Interaction between learning and development. Mind and society.* Cambridge, MA: Harvard University Press.

Walton, G. M., & Cohen, G. L. (2011). A brief social-belonging intervention improves academic and health outcomes of minority students. *Science, 331*(6023), 1447–1451.

Weisberg, D. S., & Gopnik, A. (2013). Pretense, counterfactuals, and Bayesian causal models: Why what is not real really matters. *Cognitive Science, 37,* 1368–1381.

Wigfield, A., & Eccles J. (1992). The development of achievement task values: A theoretical analysis. *Developmental Review, 12*(3), 265–310.

Winstein, C. (2014, April 9). Does practice make perfect? BrainFacts.org. Retrieved January 17, 2015, from http://www.brainfacts.org/about-neuroscience/ask-an-expert/articles/2014/does-practice-make-perfect/

Zeldin, S. (1995). *Opportunities and supports for youth development: Lessons from research and implications for community leaders and scholars.* Washington, DC: Center for Youth Development.

Zuckerman, M., Porac, J., Lathin, D., Smith, R., & Deci, E. L. (1978). On the importance of self-determination for intrinsically motivated behaviour. *Personality and Social Psychology Bulletin, 4,* 443–446.

READY TO IMPLEMENT?
HOW THE OUT-OF-SCHOOL TIME
WORKFORCE CAN SUPPORT CHARACTER
DEVELOPMENT THROUGH SOCIAL
AND EMOTIONAL LEARNING
A Review of the Literature and Future Directions

Deborah A. Moroney
American Institutes for Research

Elizabeth Devaney
University of Rochester

This paper reviews the evidence on staff practices and quality programs that foster character development through social and emotional learning. The paper describes the state of the OST workforce, and barriers and opportunities to adding social and emotional learning to their job description. Specifically, the paper provides an overview of the literature on the characteristics of staff practices that yield positive youth outcomes and the readiness of the OST workforce to implement intentional opportunities for social and emotional learning. We explore current and potential future efforts in the field to prepare staff to incorporate practices that support social and emotional learning. The paper concludes with future directions for the field and recommendations for a research agenda to explore and understand the supports for staff that ultimately foster character development through social and emotional learning. Keywords: character development, social and emotional learning, out-of-school time, afterschool, workforce, relationships.

There is a newfound interest in children's positive social and emotional development as a part of their enrichment and educational experience in both traditional PK–12 educational and out-of-school time (OST) settings. It is a newfound interest as opposed to a wholly new endeavor because the very philosophical foundation of our public education system honored the development of the whole child as a key part of the education experience (Dewey, 1916). In addition, youth development programs in OST settings have aimed to support positive development for more than 2 decades (Catalano, Berglund, Ryan, Lonczak, &

• **Correspondence concerning this article should be addressed to:** Deborah A. Moroney, dmoroney@air.org

Journal of Character Education, Volume 13(1), 2017, pp. 67–89
Copyright © 2017 Information Age Publishing, Inc.

Hawkins, 2002). More recently, there has been a flood of efforts that delineate how adults in educational and OST settings can support children's social and emotional development (Devaney, 2015b). These efforts are likely due to a combination of factors, including the following: response to good research and practice to date on children's social and emotional development and the links between positive development and academic and workforce outcomes; the backlash against accountability and standards in core content areas; and, most recently, the new language in the Every Student Succeeds Act, which honors the education of the whole child (Moroney & McGarrah, 2016).

The aforementioned "flood" of efforts to support children's social and emotional development has come in many forms and with many names: (positive) youth development, character and moral development, social and emotional learning (SEL), 21st century skills, and Foundations for Young Adult Success—among other constructs and terms to denote traits; attitudes; and skill sets such as grit, growth mindset, and noncognitive factors (Devaney, 2015b). This paper does not attempt to detangle these different but related frameworks. Instead, we discuss three framings that are especially pertinent to the OST workforce today—character, SEL, and youth development—and attempt to tease out where they overlap, service one another, or are different.

We begin with character education. Traditional character education programs were described as promoting core values and providing opportunities to practice morality in caring environments that involve families, the school, and the community (Lickona, 1996). A more modern view of character development maintains that character, among other aspects of development, is situationally driven and not fixed (i.e., it depends on the situation and the competencies the individual brings to the situation) (Nucci, 2001). Character education is defined by Character.org as the intentional practice to "support the social, emotional, and ethical development of students" (Berkowitz

& Bier, 2005). Character.org further suggests that character education programs support the development of young people's sense of fairness, responsibility, and grit, among other attitudes and skills. In order to develop these skills, character education recognizes that programs need to do more than just provide information about being socially and ethically competent—they also have to help children with how (i.e., skills) to use that knowledge to change their behavior (Elias, Parker, Kash, Weissberg, & O'Brien, 2008).

SEL is the second major framework we explore in this paper. SEL is the process by which individuals develop the attitudes, knowledge, and beliefs to succeed in school and in life. The Collaborative for Academic, Social, and Emotional Learning (CASEL) defines five core social and emotional competencies that are critical to success in school and in life: self-management, self-awareness, social awareness, relationship skills, and responsible decision making (CASEL, 2016). In school settings, SEL programs create the positive conditions (e.g., safe and supportive places, high expectations, support from adults, structured and cooperative learning environments) that ultimately contribute to children's engagement, prosocial behavior (and reduction in antisocial behavior), and academic success (Durlak, Weissberg, Dymnicki, Taylor, & Schellinger, 2011).

Finally, youth development, sometimes called *positive youth development*, is both the natural process of human development and also the strengths-based *approach* to youth-work practice (Hamilton, Hamilton, & Pittman, 2004). Youth development programs champion a strengths-based approach as opposed to a prevention mentality; they intentionally bring in family, school, and community partners to ensure programs are contextually relevant and celebrate and showcase the community's assets (Anderson-Butcher, Stetler, & Midle, 2006; Benson, 2003; Hamilton et al., 2004). Ideally, youth development programs are designed to be developmentally aligned and to provide opportunities for skill building that is embedded into the content of the program (Deschenes, McDonald, & McLaughlin, 2004; Walker, Marczak, Blyth, & Borden, 2005).

The key purpose of defining these three frameworks is to highlight that although they are not the same, all stem from common disciplines of psychology and human development. At certain points in the evolution of the implementation of each framework they reflected different educational philosophies (i.e., constructivist, behaviorist), but more recently there appears to be more common implementation practices and outcomes across frameworks, than not. That is, in some ways, SEL can be considered the *process* that helps young people to enact the *knowledge* imparted as part of character education (Elias et al., 2008). Likewise, youth development can be considered an approach to creating positive environments that ultimately support social and emotional skill building and character development. The remainder of the paper focuses on the readiness of the OST workforce to *implement SEL practices* that ultimately support participants' social and emotional skill building, including the skills needed to implement or enact key values such as respect, responsibility, and honesty that are the foundation of character development. This paper is guided by the framing question: *What are the capacity and readiness for the OST workforce to support participants' positive development, including character, through SEL?*

The first section of the paper describes youth development (also sometimes called *positive youth development* to distinguish it from the natural process of human development) as a grounding framework in OST (Hamilton et al., 2004). The paper then builds on the interrelated structures between youth development, SEL, and character, and staff members' role in these process frameworks. The paper concludes with recommendations for future practice and research to support the OST workforce in supporting participants' positive development.

QUALITY YOUTH DEVELOPMENT PROGRAMS IN OST SETTINGS

In order to frame the conversation around workforce preparedness to implement SEL, it is first important to understand the history of OST. OST programming has deep roots in a tradition of youth development. Importantly, the field has invested heavily in defining and measuring quality in youth development programs. Not surprisingly, researchers have found that participants benefit from youth development programs in OST settings when they attend regularly and the programs are implemented with quality (Durlak, Mahoney, Bohnert, & Parente, 2010; Durlak & Weissberg, 2007; Vandell, Reisner, Brown, et al., 2007; Vandell, Reisner, & Pierce, 2007). High-quality youth development programs in OST settings include some agreed-upon core components: a safe and supportive environment with contextually relevant offerings via local partnerships, in which participants have a sense of belonging, positive relationships and shared norms, and opportunities for skills building and efficacy (Kauh, 20111; Lerner et al., 2005; Phelps et al., 2007; Smith, Peck, Denault, Blazevski, & Akiva, 2010; Vandell, Reisner, Brown, et al., 2007). High-quality youth development programs allow youth participants opportunities to explore their interests, engage in learning and reflection, and build skills and knowledge (Lerner, Brittian, & Fay, 2007).

So how does youth development and its emphasis on quality instructional practices connect to the topic at hand—the development of character through SEL? Youth development is a foundational practice that encourages adults to see participants with a strengths-based lens, celebrates and includes the community, and intentionally fosters positive development through structured activities. In reviews of youth development programs, researchers have found that high-quality programs both create the conditions for and promote what are often called the *five C's* of youth development: confidence, competence, connection, caring, and *character* (Roth, Malone, & Brooks-Gunn, 2010; Lerner et al., 2005). As such, character development may be one of many possible outcomes of a high-quality youth development program. Indeed, character development has been a part of historical youth development practice and is in fact central to many youth development organizations' mission statements (e.g., YMCA, scouting, and 4-H programs). Historically, however, these organizations have not used the language of SEL to describe how they achieve this goal. That is, many programs can define what characteristics they hope their participants will have as a result of participation in their programs (e.g., be honest, respectful, have a sense of right and wrong, be empathetic, help others, etc.), but may not have had the language to articulate how youth participants have developed those characteristics. Now that the SEL framing has gained more national attention and is more accessible to nonschool programs such as those that take place in OST settings, positive youth development programs have a language and a process for how they can more intentionally support skill building and character development (i.e., through SEL practices).

OST programs are quickly adopting or claiming ownership of the language and spirit of SEL and being clear about how that work builds on other current and past efforts and frameworks. The following section further details the relationship among youth development, SEL, character development, and how that relationship is dependent on intentional and high-quality practice.

INTENTIONAL SEL PRACTICE

In 2007, amidst a flurry of activity in the field of OST to define and measure quality of structured youth development programs and to tell our OST story with sometimes misaligned academic outcome metrics, Durlak, Weissberg, and colleagues conducted a meta-analysis,

which would later become multiple CASEL reports and peer-reviewed articles in *Child Development* and the *American Journal of Community Psychology* (Durlak et al., 2007; Durlak et al., 2011; Durlak & Weissberg, 2007; Durlak, Weissberg, & Pachan, 2010). The first report, *The Impact of After-School Programs that Promote Personal and Social Skills*, outlined the findings suggesting that high-quality OST programs (1) promoted participants' development of social skills, including self-confidence, self-esteem, and bonding to school, and (2) reduced risky behaviors, which may imply sound decision making (Durlak & Weissberg, 2007). The authors specified that these outcomes were present only in high-quality programs defined as being logically and developmentally **sequenced, active** and hands on, **focused** on skill building, and **explicit** in the intention of skill building—or SAFE. This singular brief triggered not only fieldwide interest in SEL but also a sense of validation that "Yes, this is what we do in OST." Since 2007, SAFE has been twisted this way and that to fit youth development and other OST programs' definitions of quality and their implementation strategies. Most relevant has been the ongoing dialogue over whether youth development and SEL are the same, and if so, can we check the box on whether we know how to implement high-quality practices that support SEL, or not. The answer is: yes and no.

Yes, in that high-quality youth development practice and intentional SEL practices share many of the same characteristics, and both support young people's social and emotional development, including character.

However (this is the "no"), saying we already know how to do it does not do justice to our real understanding of high-quality SEL, or actually recognize what we may not yet know about high-quality SEL practice and character development in OST. Youth development programs in OST provide youth opportunities to build relationships in safe and supportive environments and to create self-determined opportunities based upon their own strengths and interests. No doubt social and emotional skill building and character development may be a consequence of this work, and for OST programs that endeavor to implement and support general positive youth development, there is no need to go further.

But for those programs in which character development and SEL are primary goals, program leaders need to identify and be intentional about how they prepare staff who are already familiar with youth development practice to extend those practices and more intentionally and concretely focus on SEL implementation.

If OST programs with a foundation of youth development are laying claim to implementing SEL and/or character development but are not intentionally implementing SEL and character development practices, then they may not be going far enough. For example, they likely aren't implementing practices with consistency, hiring prepared staff, or training existing staff to understand and implement SEL practices. Program leaders and staff need to intentionally implement SEL and character development programs, practices, or strategies if that is the goal.

Multiple studies have pointed to staff experience, preparation, characteristics, and their role in fostering positive relationships as the catalysts in implementing high-quality programs that promote positive youth outcomes

(Durlak & Weissberg, 2007; Smith et al., 2010; Vandell, 2013; Vandell & Lao, 2016). Figure 1 shows the interrelated factors that theoretically influence intentional practice in supporting SEL. Vandell (2013) suggests that the role for staff in implementing high-quality programs includes developing positive relationships, providing developmentally appropriate activities, and intentionally providing opportunities for skill building and engagement through choice and autonomous experiences. Smith and colleagues (2010) describe this relationship between setting level program quality and positive youth experience as the *point of service:* "Point of service focuses on the coexistence and correspondence between staff practices and youth experience that is likely to produce positive developmental change" (p. 359). As we train staff to intentionally support social and emotional skill building, researchers, practice leaders, and staff need to recognize that defining quality implementation for SEL and character development may be an area we need to explore more fully. The following section details the characteristics of the OST workforce and its support of young people's positive development to date.

THE OST WORKFORCE

First, who is the workforce? The OST workforce comprises almost one million individuals from a variety of preparations and back-

FIGURE 1
Interrated Factors That Influence Intentional SEL Practice

grounds from college students to parent volunteers, teachers, specialists, and youth-work professionals (Miller & Gannett, 2006; Vandell & Lao, 2016). Broadly defined, a youth worker is "an individual who works with and on behalf of children and youth to facilitate their personal, social, and educational development and enable them to gain a voice, influence, and place in society as they make the transition from dependence to independence" (Garza & Yohalem, 2013). Recent scans suggest that the OST workforce is primarily composed of young professionals (ages 18–25) and those who are retired or late career and newly entering the OST space (Vandell & Lao, 2016; Yohalem, Pittman, & Edwards, 2010). The OST workforce experiences high turnover, receives relatively low compensation for demanding work, and is staffed significantly by part-time staff (Vandell & Lao, 2016; Yohalem et al., 2010). This creates a great challenge in efforts to consistently prepare and expect staff to implement high-quality practice. It also poses a significant barrier to youth and staff forming meaningful and long-term relationships, which is critical to both high quality programming and associated social and emotional development (Vandell & Lao, 2016).

Nearly half of staff in OST programs have a 2- or 4-year degree in a variety of disciplines related to youth work, including education, child development, and social work (Vandell & Lao, 2016; Yohalem et al., 2010). A movement toward professionalizing the OST workforce currently is led by associations such as the National AfterSchool Association, the National Institute on Out-of-School Time, the National Summer Learning Association, 4-H Extension, Every Hour Counts, the Weikart Center for Youth Program Quality, and local entities such as the Partnership for Children & Youth in California and the Partnership for Afterschool Education in New York City. In addition, there is an emergence of degrees specifically focused on youth development practice at the University of Illinois at Chicago and the University of Minnesota among others, as

well as state-driven credentialing systems for child care settings. There is promise for more explicit preparation and career pathways for youth workers in the near future.

It should come as no surprise that the qualifications and motivations of the staff working in afterschool programs matter, and that high-quality programs employ staff who are "especially qualified," intrinsically motivated, and develop positive relationships with youth and families (Huang, Cho, Mostafavi, & Nam, 2008). High-quality programs have hiring practices that are structured, use formal and informal recruitment strategies, and align desired staff qualifications with needed skills (Huang et al., 2010).

Staff Preparation and Youth Engagement

Some research has found that higher levels of staff education and more structured and organized programming lead to higher levels of staff engagement, which leads to higher levels of youth engagement (Miller, 2005; Vandell, Larson, Mahoney, & Watts, 2015). For example, researchers involved in the Massachusetts After-School Research Study found a positive relationship between staff members' educational attainment and program quality indicators (e.g., youth and staff engagement), and also between staff educational attainment and participant outcomes (i.e., homework completion) (Miller, 2005). The conundrum is that the OST workforce does not have one direct educational trajectory. Few degree programs exist in youth development, SEL, character development, or related disciplines, and OST jobs do not adequately compensate individuals to pay back student loans (thus, they may not always attract an educated workforce). Traditional education pathways are one route to creating a prepared workforce, but there are other pathways. There is some evidence that staff educational level has little impact on program quality but that staff members' participation in a quality-improvement process does, suggesting that in-program professional development and reflection are paramount to supporting quality (and thus, youth outcomes, theoretically) (Smith et al., 2010). Because staff come from a variety of backgrounds and preparations, staff professional development is another feasible pathway to ensure that staff have the tools to implement high-quality opportunities for SEL. In fact, Vandell, Simzar, O'Cadiz, and Hall (2016) found a relationship between staff participation in professional development and youth participants' development of social competencies. Few studies have endeavored to make this meaningful connection between the relative value of formal postsecondary preparation, professional learning, and program quality in OST. While we do the work to influence and potentially transform postsecondary programs in the next decade to improve traditional education and OST opportunities for positive development for all young people, we can more immediately support professional learning systems and create alternate credentials that are meaningful and engaging for the adults who have such a significant impact on youth in OST programs.

For example, we may learn from the early childhood and emerging child care fields how to create multiple preparation pathways for youth work professionals. Although the OST field differs from early childhood in important ways (i.e., it is less regulated, the age range is broader, children's needs are different, the goals of OST programs are more varied), there still may be important lessons to glean from the early childhood field's decade-long focus on workforce development, quality programming, and positive child outcomes. Many states have a quality rating and improvement system for early childhood programs, which has created an infrastructure for support, both to the program quality and the workforce. Several states are currently working to integrate licensed school-age OST programs into the early childhood quality rating and improvement system in their state. In fact, the most recent Child Care Development (Block) Grant legislation includes language that suggests an increased allocation for both professional pathways and learning and quality improvement for child care settings. In some states, there are grants to support quality improvement in licensed child care settings that are part of the quality rating and improvement system, so those OST programs that serve as school-age programs and are licensed (often Boys and Girls Clubs and YMCAs, for example) may have access to professional development funds for staff.

This is an opportunity, or a moment in time, to take what we know from more than 2 decades of research and practice in early childhood and the research on the unique aspects of OST youth development, SEL, and character development to make informed decisions about how to support a workforce in implementing high-quality OST and to create meaningful and relevant career pathways for adults who make youth work a career. For example, the early childhood field has created mechanisms to foster professional learning and preparation through the Council for Professional Recognition (2016), which houses a degree registry, listings of professional learning opportunities, an online learning community, among other resources for early childhood staff; the T.E.A.C.H. Early Childhood National Center (2016) provides equitable access through funding for educational opportunities for early childhood professionals. The OST field is different from ECE, to be sure, but OST may benefit from exploring and learning from the early childhood field's structure to support ongoing professional learning and to supplement formal postsecondary opportunities to professionalize and advance the OST workforce.

THE RELATIONSHIP BETWEEN YOUTH WORKERS AND PARTICIPANTS' SOCIAL AND EMOTIONAL DEVELOPMENT

So why is the adult role in delivering high-quality programming and as an actor in positive relationships so primary to young people's social and emotional development? Why is preparation of the OST workforce to deliver SEL so essential to developing character? Despite the lack of consistent support, preparation, or remuneration for the OST workforce, we have ample evidence that staff are a key to program quality, young people's positive experience in programs, and their positive outcomes, including their social and emotional development. Staff play a critical role in the recruitment, retention, and engagement of youth in programs that ultimately support their social and emotional development. The foundations of SEL and character education, going back to social learning theory and the importance of modeling and environment in learning behavior, point to the important role adults play in supporting skill development among children (Elias et al., 2008). The following sections feature the literature on relationships among youth and staff participation in programs, staff engagement and youth engagement, and characteristics of positive relationships between youth and staff. All of these are related to participants' positive social and emotional development. Additionally, Table 1 shows results of a literature scan that includes studies of multiple OST types (structured OST and extracurricular activities) that describe, aim to change, or show effects of OST programming on participants' social and emotional development and related outcomes.

Program staff have a positive influence from the get-go on a young person's program experience. Youth are more likely to enroll in programs which there are known staff members, and are more likely to stay in programs in which staff also are returning. Furthermore, participants are more likely to enroll in and come back to programs in which they feel safe, have a sense of belonging, have choices of programming, and are engaged in activities (Vandell et al., 2015). All of the practices described here are components of OST program quality that staff members are critical players in implementing. Not surprisingly, the more youth attend programs, the more they experience the benefits of programs and, specifically

the developmental outcomes of interest (e.g., improved social skills, positive behaviors, engagement, and decrease in risky behaviors (Fredricks & Eccles, 2006; Vandell, 2013; Vandell et al., 2015). So, the more consistent staff are and the higher the quality of the programs they offer, the more youth attend and the more likely they are to experience the benefits of programming.

THE CHARACTERISTICS OF A POSITIVE RELATIONSHIP BETWEEN YOUTH AND STAFF

So where does this leave us? We know that staff who are known entities attract youth to enroll in programming, staff who stay and offer high-quality program activities retain youth in programming, and youth participation is likely to afford opportunities for positive social and emotional development. We also are aware that there are parallel structures and systems that support the workforce in early childhood. Let's focus on one aspect of quality that is especially pertinent here: the relationships between staff and youth in programs. First, we must acknowledge that adults (staff, in this case) also benefit from positive, reciprocal relationships (Lerner et al., 2006) and that when both youth and adults, or both parties in a relationship, are experiencing all of the real and perceived benefits of a relationship, they are likely to be more satisfied in their circumstance (Lerner et al., 2006). A handful of OST studies deeply explored the interactions between youth and youth workers and found that intentional, facilitated relationships between youth and youth workers were central to program quality (which we know is key in promoting youth outcomes) (Chaskin, 2009; Larson & Walker, 2010; Sullivan & Larson, 2010). In addition, Pierce, Bolt, and Vandell (2010) found that positive staff-child relationships in an OST program were associated with positive academic outcomes and increased social skills for those participants.

TABLE 1
Literature Scan of All OST Types

Reference	Study/Report Type	Program Type	Age/Grade	Staff Contribution	Youth Outcome(s)
Lerner et al. (2005)	Longitudinal Sequential Design	4-H programs, youth development organizations	Primarily Grade 5/ early adolescent	• Positive & sustained relationships with youth • Implementing activities that build important life skills • Creating opportunities for youth to use life skills as both participants in and leaders of valued community activities	• Confidence (self-worth & positive identity) • Character (personal values, social conscience, values diversity, interpersonal values & skills)
Larson & Walker (2010)	Longitudinal Design	Youth development programs; community and school-based arts & leadership programs	High school-aged youth	• Engaging responses are engaging to youth • Problems as opportunities for youth to grow/learn • Ensure that youth are incorporated into the solution • Advocate on behalf of youth	• Youth leadership • Youth engagement • Problem solving
Vandell & Lao (2016)	Research Synthesis	Afterschool programs	NA	• Must make the program appealing for youth • Caring staff, commitment to enrichment opportunities, knowledgeable, engaging • Commit to program development & self-improvement	• Develop skills & make friends • Efficacy & belonging • Social & emotional outcomes for youth
Vandell et al. (2015)	Research Synthesis	Afterschool programs, OST settings, including extracurricular activities, camps, museum & library programs	NA	• Strong relationship with youth participants • Ensure youth feel safe, have a sense of belonging, & feel there are opportunities to develop for the future • Offer freely chosen, enjoyable-for-youth activities	• Positive self-perceptions • Positive social behaviors & positive relationships with peers • Noncognitive skills (persistence, teamwork, emotional regulation) • Change in problem behaviors (truancy, delinquent acts)
Vandell (2016)	Quasi-experimental Design	Afterschool programs, focused on STEM	Primarily elementary	• Strong beliefs in the importance of STEM activities • Strong efficacy when implementing STEM activities • Participated in professional development	• Social competency (in relationships with peers)

(Table continues on next page.)

TABLE 1
(Continued)

Reference	Study/Report Type	Program Type	Age/Grade	Staff Contribution	Youth Outcome(s)
Hall, Yohalem, Toleman, & Wilson (2003)	Qualitative Design	Afterschool programs	Varied	• Positive relationships with youth (guidance; interest in youth; be responsive, attentive, & nonjudgmental) • Youth development at center of organizational development • High expectations for youth participants • Hold youth to clear standards & affirm youths' potential • Implement activities with inclusive opportunities for youth to demonstrate new skills & receive feedback • Make sure youth have a feeling of choice	• Connections with caring, encouraging staff • Positive relationships with peers • Autonomy and self-direction
Vandell (2013)	Research Synthesis	Afterschool programs	NA	• Develop positive relationships with youth for youth & peers • Developmental activities that develop youth skill sets • Promote youth engagement • Work toward youth obtaining skills & knowledge • Provide structure, with opportunity for choice	• Autonomy • Positive behavioral outcomes (increased social skills with peers, prosocial behavior, engagement) • Change in behavior seen as destructive (aggression, misconduct)
Vandell, Reisner, Brown, et al. (2007)	Multicity Quasi-experimental Design	Afterschool programs	Elementary and middle school youth	• Provide youth physical & emotional safety, structure, positive relationships with peers; establish social norms • Foster partnership among the program, school, families, & community • Build a positive environment (engages youth, opportunities for growth, leadership, independence)	• Prosocial behaviors & social skills • Reduction in aggressive behaviors
Morrissey & Werner-Wilson (2005)	Quasi-experimental Design	School-based extracurricular activities, religious activities, community-based clubs, sports, service groups	Ages 10–18	• Ensure that activities promote prosocial values • Build leadership & problem-solving skills • Implement hands-on & cooperative activities • Engagement with family & community	• Prosocial behavior

(Table continues on next page.)

TABLE 1
(Continued)

Reference	Study/Report Type	Program Type	Age/Grade	Staff Contribution	Youth Outcome(s)
Fredricks & Eccles (2006)	Longitudinal Sample Quasi-experimental Design	Various school-based extracurricular activities	Grades 7–12	• Provide guidance as supportive adult mentors • Create opportunities for youth to feel they belong • Have age-appropriate program structure • Implement challenging & meaningful activities • Create opportunities for skill building	• Positive peer relationships • Self-worth
Riggs, Jahromi, Razza, Dillworth, & Mueller (2006)	Research Synthesis	School-based afterschool academic achievement & social skills program	Grades 1–6	• Provide a safe environment for youth • Create opportunities for building social competencies	• Social competencies • Change in problem behaviors
Mahoney, Cairns, & Farmer (2003)	Longitudinal Sample Quasi-experimental Design	Various school-based extracurricular activities	Grades 4–7	• Form positive relationship with youth • Ensure youth build positive relationships with peers	• Interpersonal competence in middle adolescence • Strong relationships with peers • Change in risky behavior
Ettekal, Callina, & Lerner (2015)	Research Synthesis	Organized activities	Grade 7	• Ensure youth are respected • Positive relationship between staff & youth • Foster positive relationship among peers • Encourage youth to participate in key decisions & demonstrate respect by showing interest in youth	• Respect for adults & staff from youth • Respect for other cultures • Positive social interactions with peers
Jagers (2001)	Research Synthesis	School-based social & emotional competency building programs, extra hour of afterschool time	NA	• Model moral competencies • Provide leadership development opportunities, cultural empowerment • Daily social & emotional learning modules	• Social & emotional competency • Moral self-efficacy • Prosocial behavior with peers • Self-control

What do these positive relationships look like? They are characterized by shared norms, high expectations, stability and continuity, and connectedness to each other's lives (e.g., school, community, family) (Hall et al., 2003; Vandell, Reisner, Brown et al., 2007). The positive outcomes associated with positive adult/youth relationships has been well studied in traditional education settings, and specifically when adults have high expectations of the youth with whom they work. A longitudinal study of middle school students found that youth who reported that their teachers had a positive perception of them had increased academic success, increased self-esteem, and decreased anger (Roeser & Eccles, 1998). In addition to high expectations, staff are successful in creating positive relationships with participants when they are respectful; provide youth with guidance; show a genuine interest in youth; and are responsive, attentive, and nonjudgmental (Ettekal et al., 2015; Hall et al., 2003). In OST settings, organizational development and staff practices should be grounded in a core philosophy of youth development to foster positive and respectful relationships (Deschenes et al., 2004; Hall et al., 2003).

We have learned that staff need to be educated in a related degree or prepared and continually provided opportunities for professional development *and* engaged *and* that they need to stay in low-paying, high-demand jobs. They need to implement high-quality programs that reflect youth interests and to be in partnerships with the family and community. All the while, they need to do so with the utmost care and responsiveness to ensure that all participants feel safe and have a strong sense of belonging, have opportunities to form positive relationships and practice skill and knowledge building in any number of content areas, and have opportunities for efficacy and leadership. Now, we are saying they should be ensuring that participants have explicit opportunities for SEL in order to support their positive development and character. This is a tall order. Let's consider whether the OST workforce is ready to implement SEL.

READINESS TO IMPLEMENT

As a field, are we ready to support the OST workforce as it develops this next layer of expertise? Are members of the OST workforce ready and prepared to implement programs that support participants' social and emotional development, including character? In 2015, the National AfterSchool Association conducted a scan of its members, asking them to respond to questions focused on their value, interest, ability, expertise, and needs in implementing OST opportunities that supported SEL. Not surprisingly, the findings suggested that OST programs place a high value on SEL and report implementing opportunities for SEL, but responses were mixed on whether staff felt equipped to implement SEL. The majority of respondents indicated that they wanted more resources and professional development on SEL (National AfterSchool Association & American Institutes for Research, 2016). Across the country, PK–12 education systems, schools, and OST programs are endeavoring not only to implement opportunities for SEL and character development but also to assess social and emotional competencies. It is critical that we take stock of where we are in OST organizational practices that support staff and their implementation of SEL, program implementation, and the readiness and comfort level of staff in implementing SEL.

The National AfterSchool Association, along with the National Institute on Out-of-School Time, has developed core knowledge and competencies for afterschool and youth development professionals (National AfterSchool Association, 2011). Intermediary organizations have recently designed tools to support staff member implementation of SEL, reflect on SEL practice, and determine their readiness to assess social and emotional development (Devaney, 2015a; Moroney & McGarrah, 2016; Smith, McGovern, Larson, Hillaker, & Peck, 2016). These resources only scratch the surface if they are not accompanied by organizational buy-in, ongoing and aligned professional development, and staff inclusion and readiness for this new endeavor. We know from research that adoption of new practices at scale—or "diffusion of innovation" in research speak—is most effective when the problem is visible or tangible, when the solution is doable (e.g., requires small effort on the part of the individual or is relatively simple), and when the innovation or new practice has been tested and is supported by peers (Gawande, 2013; Rogers, Singhal, &

Quinlan, 2009). Coburn (2003) suggests that bringing an education initiative to scale requires more than just putting it in lots of classrooms—it requires a depth and spread of implementation that gets to the core of the ideas by changing norms and beliefs, not just activities, by getting people on the ground involved in solving the problem. Something similar needs to happen with the OST field. SEL and related practices need to be made relevant to the workforce; the language and practices need to be made accessible; and the OST workforce needs to be meaningfully engaged in defining high-quality SEL in OST settings in order for successful and widespread adoption of SEL practice and character development. Efforts are underway to this effect. American Institutes for Research has released a variety of tools and briefs designed to help practitioners with how to implement and assess their own SEL practice. Likewise, the Susan Crown Exchange and the Weikart Center for Youth Program Quality, through their SEL Challenge, have developed a guide for programs serving older youth on how to incorporate SEL practices into OST programming. But much more is needed to help the OST workforce truly understand SEL practice and how it plays a role in improving social, emotional, and character development.

FUTURE DIRECTIONS
FOR OST PRACTICE:
A NEW JOB DESCRIPTION

At this juncture, we may consider how we can support staff in implementing SEL, while at the same time avoiding the youth work pivot. Over the years, we have asked youth workers to be instant specialists in prevention programming; arts; environmental education; literacy; academic enrichment and Supplemental Education Services; Science, Technology, Engineering, and Mathematics; and life skills, to name a few. Staff who are primarily part time and with low pay have had to pivot from one important initiative to another, often with little

preparation or background, and, as such have experienced trend fatigue with each new and important initiative. Throughout this time, our pervasive mission has been to support children and youth in their positive development. As we explore, identify, and implement practices to support staff in their preparation to implement high-quality SEL and character development, we need to acknowledge: (1) this effort builds on the OST field's fundamental mission of supporting youth development, and (2) if the goal of a program is to support content development (e.g., arts exploration), then it may not be necessary for the entire program to make a shift to SEL. An entire content-varied and rich field does not all have to simultaneously pivot to a new mission and content—only one that makes sense for an organization in its history, context, and future direction.

Perhaps we don't need to redefine the role of every youth worker in a way that makes SEL yet one more thing they need to learn and be able to "do." Perhaps instead, we need to think about SEL practice as we might any other important skills we seek in employees. Take, for example, communication. Just about every job description talks about the importance of communication skills for success. Usually, to do your job well, you need to be able to communicate with other staff, clients, or key stakeholders. But for some, communication is more a key component of the job than others—a marketing director at a company must have greater communication skills than, say, the computer programmer. Both may need it, but the one as part of their overall effectiveness as an employee and the other as a core component of the work of their job. What if we did the same for youth workers? Everyone needs to understand and support SEL as an overall part of their job, but we can make a new job description for youth workers who specialize in SEL. This role would be similar to academic liaisons who connect the OST program with in-school learning and ensure that activities are aligned and working in conjunction with the school. A youth worker focused on SEL would ensure that programming is infused with both embedded and explicit SEL practices. This approach presents not only the opportunity for programs to have SEL-focused staff members but also another career trajectory for youth workers.

The following recommendations for next steps represent the collective thinking of field leaders on future directions in research and practice. Building on the core question presented in the introduction of this paper, we asked field leaders: *What is the next step in the field to prepare the OST workforce to support participants' character development through SEL?* The following themes emerged from their responses.

Organizational Support Toward Sustainability

Youth-serving organizations, schools, and other agencies that house OST programs should support the value of SEL from the outset of programming. There needs to be organizational buy-in, including supportive adults, to foster settings that promote positive development and to invest resources in the supports that staff need (e.g., professional development) to learn or bolster SEL strategies. Before making a shift to SEL, organizations must consider sustainability of organizational support for SEL in consideration of the issues of staff turnover previously mentioned in this paper. Organizations also may consider how they will evaluate the effectiveness of staff practice in implementing SEL. There exists great controversy around using youth-level measures of social and emotional competence to gauge staff practice. At the same time, we know that continuous-quality-improvement practices that include staff reflection on their own implementation lead to improved quality programming and staff engagement.

Adoption of Frameworks and Knowing What That Means

There are two lines of thinking on adopting a common framework and language to describe the process of SEL and associated

outcomes of social and emotional competencies, with the framing of workforce preparation for implementing high-quality SEL. First, there are some who assert that we need to agree on a common framework and shared understanding of language. Second, others are comfortable with "locally" adopted frameworks. At the very least, there must be consensus *within* a program, or system of programs, in which staff may have job mobility, that there be a common framework and clarity of language. This very article points to the complexity of language. SEL and character education are two frameworks with some common goals and strategies, but staff who are asked to contribute to, understand, and practice both may be confused. There are efforts underway in both in-school and OST SEL to move toward consensus building for a variety of reasons, but most primarily to detangle and clarify strategies for staff and buy-in from stakeholders.

Culture and Context

We need to explicitly explore and critically address issues of cultural bias. SEL and character are culturally defined and may function differently in different contexts. Character, in particular, is laden with contextual implications because many consider character within a religious framing or a context of "right" and "wrong." These terms can be understood differently in different contexts, and we need to do more than just acknowledge this challenge. We need to start having the critical conversations about the appropriateness, relevance, and application of SEL and character in a variety of OST programs serving a wide variety of people. We not only need to pay credence and attention to this space, but we also need to start having conversations that include youth, family members, staff, and community members on the strategies and competencies that are relevant and valued by a community. Moreover, we need to pay attention to how different contexts (e.g., a small program, a rural program) influence opportunities for staff to implement high-quality SEL and how high-quality SEL is defined in those contexts. The Asia Society and Policy Studies Associates are leading a coideation process around 21st century competencies with systems builders across the globe (Stewart, 2015). This may be one method to ensure the relevance of efforts to support SEL and aligned staff supports as we move forward in creating a more responsive and culturally reflective approach to SEL and character development across contexts.

Adult Social and Emotional Competence

The OST workforce has a wide and varied job description. Not unlike other fields today, we know we have to add social and emotional competencies to the job qualifications list. Studies show that employers want these skills, above almost all others, and that we cannot teach young people to change their behavior if we are not able to model how to do it ourselves (American Management Association, 2012; Elias et al., 2007). We want OST staff to know themselves and to be able to work well with others by being good communicators and collaborators. These are all core competencies of a good employee, team player, and someone who can form ongoing and positive relationships that are critical to young people's positive experience in OST and positive development. We also expect staff to be able to role-model social and emotional competencies (and the strategies for SEL, such as reflection) with youth and colleagues in their programming. This additional expectation of the workforce may be a cumbersome hiring shift for some organizations that have historically hired a steady stream of part-time staff members with varying levels of youth-work experience and education. This new goal (not just in the OST workforce) to shift not only to an experienced and prepared workforce but also to an experienced, prepared, *and* socially and emotionally competent workforce will take time and careful thought, because in the end, we are all developing and can use support in our ongoing positive development. Building off the previous topic of explicitly addressing cul-

ture and context in OST programs, we also need staff voice in this conversation to acknowledge staff members' experience with SEL; the contexts in which they live, work, and play; and how their background and culture contribute to their practice. In the short term, ensuring that the OST workforce is meaningfully engaged in the conversation around SEL and its relevance, and aware that their social and emotional competence influences their work, the quality of programs, and young people's experience is a feasible and very important first step.

Professional Learning and Development

Messaging is critical to professional development for the OST workforce. There appears to be confusion in the field on terminology and frameworks, and SEL has been misconstrued as a completely new concept when in fact there are many similarities among them. To avoid the dogma of another new thing, and the associated youth work pivot, we may consider messaging that SEL is youth development done really well, with additional intentional practice to foster social and emotional skill building and facilitate character development.

This paper presents an overview of the varied formal and informal preparation that OST staff, in addition to their own intrinsic strengths and interests, bring to programs. To professionalize the OST workforce, the OST field should support, design, and implement varied and ongoing professional learning and development for OST on awareness and strategies to implement SEL in OST settings. Staff will come with varying levels of experience, resources, and prior knowledge in SEL. In an effort to address this variety, professional learning opportunities may vary by model of delivery (coaching, technical assistance, workshops, online tools and resources such as communities of practice and UCourses, shared resources, and examples of best practice) and by method of transfer (online, in person, resource sharing) to address not only diversity of experience but also learning style, and to accommodate the often part-time workforce. OST programs also should consider program participants, context, and offerings to contextualize training. For example, staff who work with youth from prekindergarten through middle school may participate in professional learning that is offered by developmental stage. Programs that are offered in conjunction with other supports for youth and families should include professional learning opportunities on how programs and initiatives align and how to collaborate toward shared goals. Common agreement on a framework, language, and reflective buy-in are all a priori to professional development; otherwise, it may end up being confusing, dismissed, or—in the worst case—disrespectful.

Intentionality

Likely, one of the most important next steps for the field of OST and, ultimately, the workforce is to define and understand intentional SEL practice. Broadly defined, intentional practice is the purposeful implementation of practices and strategies to support SEL and character (as opposed to general quality practices that may result in SEL and character). Intentional practices also are responsive to the developmental stage of youth in the program, their readiness to learn, and the culture and context of the program and community (Deschenes et al., 2004). The development of such intentional practices can be done program by program by planning activities based on information continually gathered from participants via focus groups, surveys, interviews, and other forms of informal communication. Intentional activities are designed to be open to and inclusive of youth, family, and community voice in programming. As noted previously, the field has a history and systems to support quality practice that may result in positive youth development outcomes, but we have yet to adequately define and adopt SEL practices that support character development and other social and emotional outcomes by develop-

mental stage, in a variety of contexts, and that reflect, respect, and honor cultural diversity.

Connections to Other Fields

The OST workforce is not alone in its exploration of and preparation to implement SEL practices. As a result of a multitude of factors—including the groundswell of interest and support for SEL in PK–12 settings and the recent Every Student Succeeds Act—the field of education is also grappling with the issue of both local and scaled implementation of SEL and preparing teachers to implement practices that support SEL in schools. Similarly, higher education and workforce development programs are eager to define and support skills pathways to ensure today's children are prepared for tomorrow's jobs. Ideally, the fields of OST, PK–12 education, higher education institutions, and those who support workforce readiness may come together both to define the interrelated skills pathways that exist between fields and to collaboratively prepare a more generalized education and OST workforce that have a shared understanding of SEL and implementation of practices that support social and emotional development.

FUTURE DIRECTIONS FOR OST: A RESEARCH AGENDA

There is still much we do not know about implementation of SEL in OST, how SEL can support or align with character development, and the OST workforce in general. This paper references basic research, scans, commentary, and collective voices for next steps in practice and research. The following proposed research questions are based upon the gaps identified in this paper, and field leaders' recommendations for further research. The research questions fall into three main categories: implementation studies, studies on the characteristics of the workforce, and impacts of SEL programming on adults.

Implementation Studies on SEL Practice in OST

The following are example research questions:

- What does high-quality SEL practice look like?
- What are levers of implementation uptake at the program and staff levels?
- How do uptake and practice vary in different contexts and within and across cultures?
- What are the relationships between implementation of high-quality SEL and other practices?
- How can SEL support or align with other frameworks (e.g., character education) in a way that honors founding principles on all sides?

Studies on the OST Workforce

Some example research questions are as follows:

- What is the OST workforces' current knowledge on SEL, character development, and related frameworks and how they interact and relate to one another?
- What are the factors (e.g., buy-in, confidence, comfort level) that influence staff in their implementation and uptake of SEL in OST?
- What (resources, professional learning) does the OST workforce need in order to implement high-quality SEL practice?
- What methods of professional development are most impactful on SEL practice?

Studies on the Impacts of Implementing High Quality SEL Practice

Example research questions include the following:

- How does implementing high-quality SEL impact job satisfaction and retention?
- How does implementing high-quality SEL translate to adult practice? How does it change adult SEL skills—do staff who learn and implement SEL become more socially and emotionally competent themselves?
- Do staff in OST settings identify more with one framework (e.g., character education, moral development, youth development) over another, and how does SEL implementation change that understanding?

Finally, it is clear that we need to include youth, staff, and family voice in defining both practice and the resulting research agenda around high-quality OST and intentional SEL practices and resulting outcomes. This will ensure that both practice and research approaches are relevant and respect differences. Research can support the OST field and their workforce by studying the value of different forms of workforce preparation on SEL initiatives, and in building the knowledge base around high-quality SEL practice in OST. As a field, we need to come together around terminology and expectations, and to ensure that the resulting messages are clear, relevant, and accessible. The OST workforce is primed for supporting character development through SEL in OST programs but needs significant support in terms of resources, professional learning, and creating professional pathways.

Also, in support of staff, the OST field should remember that supporting young people's positive development is not new, but that implementing intentional opportunities for SEL does merit further definition and support. OST staff will champion SEL in support of participants' social and emotional development, including character development, if we can honor and build upon decades of good work instead of suggesting it is yet another pivot. As LL Cool J says, "Don't call it a comeback: We've been here for years" (Smith, 1990).

REFERENCES

American Management Association. (2012). AMA 2012 critical skills survey. New York, NY: Author. Retrieved from http://www.amanet.org/uploaded/2012-CriticalSkills-Survey.pdf

Anderson-Butcher, D., Stetler, E. G., & Midle, T. (2006). A case for expanded school-community partnerships in support of positive youth development. *Children & Schools, 28*(3), 155–163.

Benson, P. L. (2003). Developmental assets and asset-building community: Conceptual and empirical foundations. In R. M. Lerner & P. L. Benson (Eds.)., *Developmental assets and asset building communities: Implications for research, policy and practice* (pp. 19–43). Norwell, MA: Kluwer.

Berkowitz, M. W., & Bier, M. C. (2005). *What works in character education: A research-driven guide for educators.* Washington, DC: Character Education Partnership.

Catalano, R. F., Berglund, M. L., Ryan, J. A. M., Lonczak, H. S., & Hawkins, J. D. (2002). Positive youth development in the United States: Research findings on evaluations of positive youth development programs. *Prevention and Treatment, 5*, 1–104.

Chaskin, R. J. (2009). Toward a theory of change in community-based practice with youth: A case-study exploration. *Children & Youth Services Review, 31*(10), 1127–1134.

Coburn, C. E. (2003). Rethinking scale: Moving beyond numbers to deep and lasting change. *Educational Researcher, 32*(6), 3–12.

Collaborative for Academic, Social, and Emotional Learning. (2016). *Social and emotional learning core competencies.* Retrieved from http://www.casel.org/social-and-emotional-learning/core-competencies/

Council for Professional Recognition. (2016). Home page. Retrieved from http://www.cdacouncil.org

Deschenes, S., McDonald, M., & McLaughlin, M., (2004). Youth organizations: From principles to practice. In S. F. Hamilton & M. A. Hamilton (Eds.), *The youth development handbook: Coming of age in American communities* (pp. 25–50). Thousand Oaks, CA: SAGE.

Devaney, E. (2015a). *Social and emotional learning practices: A self-reflection tool for afterschool staff.* Washington, DC: American Institutes for Research. Retrieved from http://www.air.org/resource/social-and-emotional-learning-practices-self-reflection-tool-afterschool-staff

Devaney, E. (2015b). *Supporting social and emotional development through quality afterschool programs.* Washington, DC: American Institutes for Research.

Dewey, J. (1916). *Democracy and education: An introduction to the philosophy of education.* New York, NY: Macmillan.

Durlak, J., Dymnicki, A. B., Taylor, R. D., Weissberg, R., & Schellinger, K. B. (2011). The impact of enhancing students' social and emotional learning: A meta-analysis of school-based universal interventions. *Child Development, 82*(1), 405–432.

Durlak, J. A., Mahoney, J. L., Bohnert, A. M., & Parente, M. E. (2010). Developing and improving after-school programs to enhance youth's personal growth and adjustment: A special issue of AJCP. *American Journal of Community Psychology, 45*, 285–293.

Durlak, J. A., Taylor, R. D., Kawashima, K., Pachan, M. K., DuPre, E. P., Celio, C. I., … Weissberg, R. P. (2007). Effects of positive youth development programs on school, family, and community systems. *American Journal of Community Psychology, 39*(3–4), 269–286.

Durlak, J. A., & Weissberg, R. P. (2007). *The impact of after-school programs that promote personal and social skills.* Chicago, IL: Collaborative for Academic, Social, and Emotional Learning.

Durlak, J. A., Weissberg, R. P., & Pachan, M. (2010). A meta-analysis of after-school programs that seek to promote personal and social skills in children and adolescents. *American Journal of Community Psychology, 45*, 294–309.

Elias, M. J., Parker, S. J., Kash, V. M., Weissberg, R. P., & O'Brien, M. U. (2008). Social and emotional learning, moral education, and character education: A comparative analysis and a view toward convergence. In L. P. Nucci & D. Narvaez (Eds.), *Handbook of moral and character education* (pp. 248–266). New York, NY: Routledge

Ettekal, A. V., Callina, K. S., & Lerner, R. M. (2015). The promotion of character through youth development programs: A view of the issues. *Journal of Youth Development, 10*(3), 6–13.

Fredricks, J. A., & Eccles, J. S. (2006). Extracurricular involvement and adolescent adjustment: Impact of duration, number of activities, and breadth of participation. *Applied Developmental Science, 10*(3), 132–146.

Garza, P., & Yohalem, N. (2013). *What is the next generation youth work coalition?* (Definition of a youth worker, p. 2). Retrieved from www.niost.org/pdf/Coalition%20Description.pdf

Gawande, A. (2013, July 29). Slow ideas. *The New Yorker.* Retrieved from https://www.newyorker.com/magazine/2013/07/29/slow-ideas

Hall, G., Yohalem, N., Toleman, J., & Wilson, A. (2003). *How afterschool programs can most effectively promote positive youth development as a support to academic achievement.* Wellesley, MA: National Institute on Out-of-School Time. Retrieved from https://4-h.org/wp-content/uploads/2016/02/WCW3.pdf

Hamilton, S. F., Hamilton, M. A., & Pittman, K. D. (2004). Principles for youth development. In S. F. Hamilton & M. A. Hamilton (Eds.), *The youth development handbook: Coming of age in American communities* (pp. 3–22). Thousand Oaks, CA: SAGE.

Huang, D., Cho, J., Mostafavi, S., & Nam, H. (2008). *What works? Common practices in high functioning afterschool programs: The National Partnership for Quality Afterschool Learning final report.* Austin, TX: SEDL. Retrieved from http://www.sedl.org/afterschool/commonpractices.pdf

Huang, D., Cho, J., Nam, H., La Torre, D., Oh, C., Harven, A., ... Caverly, S. (2010). *Examining practices of staff recruitment and retention in four high-functioning afterschool programs* (CRESST Report 769). Los Angeles: University of California, National Center for Research on Evaluation, Standards, and Student Testing. Retrieved from https://www.cse.ucla.edu/products/reports/R769.pdf

Jagers, R. J. (2001). Cultural integrity and social and emotional competence promotion: Work notes on moral competence. *The Journal of Negro Education, 70*(1/2), 59–71.

Kauh, T. (2011). *AfterZone: Outcomes for youth participating in Providence's citywide after-school system.* Philadelphia, PA: Public/Private Ventures. Retrieved from http://www.wallacefoundation.org/knowledge-center/Documents/AfterZone-Outcomes-Youth-Participating-Providences-Citywide-After-School-System.pdf

Larson, R., & Walker, K. (2010). Dilemmas of practice: Challenges to program quality encountered by youth program leaders. *American Journal of Community Psychology, 45*(3), 338–349.

Lerner, R. M., Brittian, A., & Fay, K. (2007). Mentoring: A key resource for promoting positive youth development. *Research in Action, 1*, 3–5.

Lerner, R. M., Lerner, J. V., Almerigi, J. B., Theokas, C., Phelps, E., Gestsdottir, S., ... von Eye, A. (2005). Positive youth development, participation in community youth development programs, and community contributions of fifth-grade adolescents: Findings from the first wave of the 4-H study of positive youth development. *Journal of Early Adolescence, 25*(1), 17–71.

Lerner, R. M., Lerner, J. V., Almerigi, J., Theokas, C., Phelps, E., Naudeau, S., ... von Eye, A. (2006). Towards a new vision and vocabulary about adolescence: Theoretical, empirical, and applied bases of a "positive youth development" perspective. In L. Balter & C. S. Tamis-LeMonda (Eds.), *Child psychology: A handbook of contemporary issues* (pp. 445–469). New York, NY: Psychology Press/Taylor & Francis.

Lickona, T. (1996). Eleven principles of effective character education. *Journal of Moral Education, 25*(1), 93–100.

Mahoney, J. L., Cairns, B. D., & Farmer, T. W. (2003). Promoting interpersonal competence and educational success through extracurricular activity participation. *Journal of Educational Psychology, 95*, 409–418.

Miller, B. M. (2005). *Pathways to success for youth: What counts in after-school.* Wellesley, MA: National Institute on Out-of-School Time.

Miller, B., & Gannett, E. (2006). Who is the afterschool workforce? *Evaluation Exchange, 11*(4). Retrieved from http://www.hfrp.org/evaluation/the-evaluation-exchange/issue-archive/professional-development/who-is-the-afterschool-workforce

Moroney, D., & McGarrah, M. (2016, January 29). *Are you ready to assess social and emotional development?* (SEL Solutions Brief). Washington, DC: American Institutes for Research. Retrieved from http://www.air.org/sites/default/files/AIR%20Ready%20to%20Assess_STOP.pdf

Morrissey, K. M., & Werner-Wilson, R. J. (2005). The relationship between out-of-school activities and positive youth development: An investigation of the influences of communities and family. *Adolescence, 40*(157), 67–85.

National AfterSchool Association and American Institutes for Research. (2016). *Building on a strong foundation.* McLean, VA: National After-School Association

National AfterSchool Association. (2011). *Core knowledge and competencies for afterschool and youth development professionals* (2nd ed.). McLean, VA: Author. Retrieved from http://naaweb.org/images/pdf/NAA_Final_Print.pdf

Nucci, L. (2001). *Education in the moral domain.* Cambridge, England: Cambridge University Press.

Phelps, E., Balsano, A. B., Fay, K., Peltz, J. S., Zimmerman, S. M, Lerner, R. M., & Lerner, J. V. (2007). Nuances in early adolescent development trajectories of positive and of problematic/risk behaviors: Findings from the 4-H Study of positive youth development. In N. Carrey & M. Ungar (Eds.), Resilience in children and youth [Special Issue]. *Child and Adolescent Clinics of North America, 16*(2), 473–496.

Pierce, K., Bolt, D., & Vandell, D. (2010). Specific features of after-school program quality: Associations with children's functioning in middle childhood. *American Journal of Community Psychology, 45*(3–4), 381–393.

Riggs, N. R., Jahromi, L. B., Razza, R. P., Dillworth, J. E., & Mueller, U. (2006). Executive function and the promotion of social-emotional competence. *Journal of Applied Developmental Psychology, 27,* 300–309.

Roeser, R. W., & Eccles, J. S. (1998). Adolescents' perceptions of middle school: Relation to longitudinal changes in academic and psychological adjustment. *Journal of Research on Adolescence, 8*(1), 123–158.

Rogers, E. M., Singhal, A., & Quinlan, M.M. (2009). Diffusion of Innovations. In D. W. Stacks & M. B. Salwen (Eds.), *An integrated approach to communication theory and research* (2nd ed., pp. 418–434). New York, NY: Routledge.

Roth, J., Malone, L., & Brooks-Gunn, J. (2010). Does the amount of participation in afterschool programs relate to developmental outcomes? A review of the literature. *American Journal of Community Psychology, 45*(3), 310–324.

Smith, J. S. (1990). Mama said knock you out [Recorded by LL Cool J]. On *Mama said knock you out* [CD]. New York, NY: Def Jam Recordings. (September 14, 1990)

Smith, C., McGovern, G., Larson, R., Hillaker, B., & Peck., S. C. (2016). *Preparing youth to thrive: Promising practices in social emotional learning.* Washington, DC: Forum for Youth Investment.

Smith, C., Peck, S., Denault, A., Blazevski, J., & Akiva, T. (2010). Quality at the point of service: Profiles of practice in after-school settings. *American Journal of Community Psychology, 45*(3), 358–369.

Stewart, V. (2015). Preparing students for the 21st century: International strategies. Retrieved from http://asiasociety.org/global-cities-education-network/preparing-students-21st-century

Sullivan, P. J., & Larson, R. W. (2010). Connecting youth to high-resource adults: Lessons from effective youth programs. *Journal of Adolescent Research, 25*(1), 99–123.

T.E.A.C.H. Early Childhood® National Center. (2016). Results and reports. Retrieved from http://teachecnationalcenter.org/center-initiatives-and-resources/results-and-reports/

Vandell, D. L. (2013). Afterschool program quality and student outcomes: Reflections on key findings from recent research. In T. K. Peterson (Ed.) *Expanding minds and opportunities: leveraging the power of afterschool and summer learning for student success.* Washington, DC: Collaborative Communications Group. Retrieved from http://www.expandinglearning.org/expandingminds

Vandell, D., & Lao, J. (2016). Building and retaining high quality professional staff for extended education programs. *International Journal for Research on Extended Education, 4*(1), 52–64.

Vandell, D. L., Larson, R., Mahoney, J., & Watts, T. (2015). Children's organized activities. In R. Lerner (Series Ed.) and M. H. Bornstein & T. Leventhal (Volume Eds.), *Handbook of child psychology and developmental science: Vol. 4. Ecological settings and processes in developmental systems* (7th ed., pp. 305–344). New York, NY: Wiley Inter-science.

Vandell, D., Reisner, E., Brown, B., Pierce, K., Dadisman, K., & Pechman, E. (2007). *The study of promising after-school programs: Descriptive report of the promising programs.* Flint, MI: Charles Stewart Mott Foundation.

Vandell, D. L., Reisner, E. R., Pierce, K. M. (2007). *Outcomes linked to high-quality afterschool programs: Longitudinal findings from the study of promising afterschool programs.* Washington, DC: Policy Studies Associates.

Vandell, D., Simzar, R., O'Cadiz, P. & Hall, V. (2016). Findings from an afterschool STEM learning initiative. *Journal of Expanded Learning Opportunities, 1*(3), 7–26.

Walker, J., Marczak, M., Blyth, D., & Borden, L. (2005). Designing youth development programs: Toward a theory of developmental intentional-ity. In J. L. Mahoney, R. W. Larson, & J. S. Eccles (Eds.), *Organized activities as contexts of development* (pp. 399–418). Mahwah, NJ: Erlbaum.

Yohalem, N., Pittman, K., & Edwards, S. L. (2010). *Strengthening the youth development/after-school workforce: Lessons learned and implications for funders.* Washington, DC: Forum for Youth Investment. Retrieved from http://forumfyi.org/files/Strengthening_the_YD-AS_Workforce.pdf

CPSIA information can be obtained
at www.ICGtesting.com
Printed in the USA
FSOW02n2231060118
42976FS